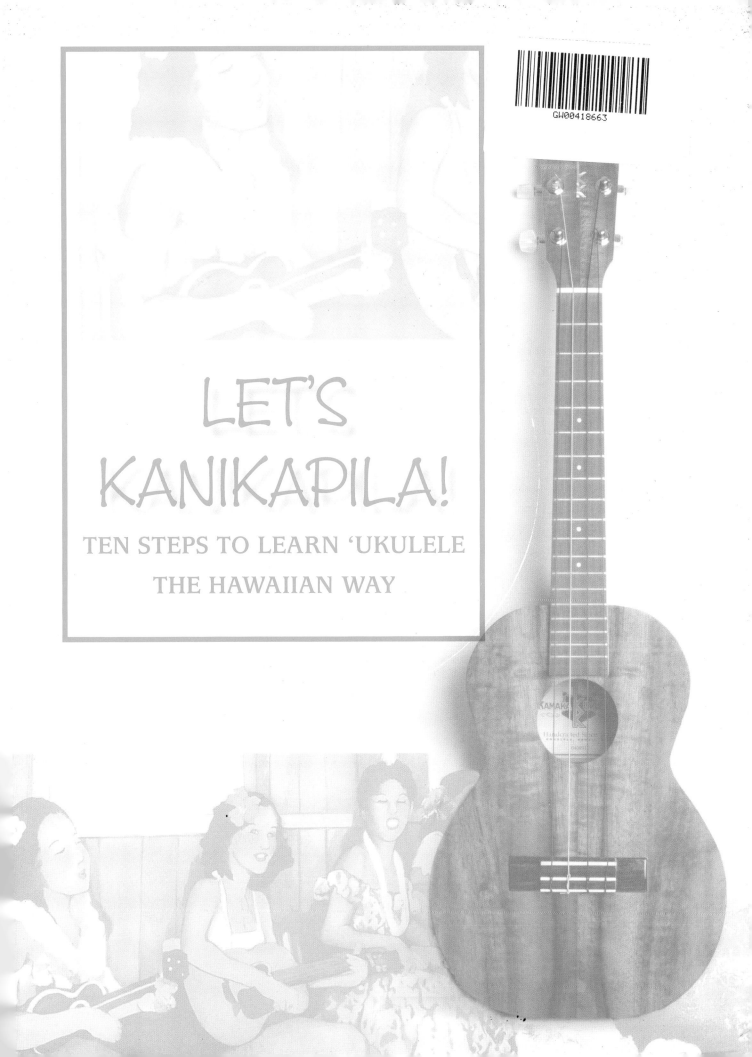

LET'S KANIKAPILA!

TEN STEPS TO LEARN 'UKULELE

THE HAWAIIAN WAY

LET'S KANIKAPILA!

TEN STEPS TO LEARN 'UKULELE

THE HAWAIIAN WAY

Michael Preston

Mutual Publishing

LCCN: 2006930137
ISBN-10: 1-56647-806-5
ISBN-13: 978-1-56647-806-9

Design by Wanni

First Printing, September 2006
Second Printing, June 2007
Third Printing, March 2008
Fourth Printing, April 2010
Fifth Printing, January 2012

Mutual Publishing, LLC
1215 Center Street, Suite 210
Honolulu, Hawai'i 96816
Ph: 808-732-1709 / Fax: 808-734-4094
email: info@mutualpublishing.com
www.mutualpublishing.com

Printed in Korea

TABLE OF CONTENTS

ALPHABETICAL LIST OF PERFORMANCE REPERTOIRE

FOREWORD

Dear Teachers and Students of 'Ukulele,

It is my pleasure to introduce you to this exciting new resource for teaching and learning 'ukulele.

I have known and worked with Michael Preston, the author of this book, for the past six years as a consultant and colleague in the Honolulu Waldorf School. His hard work and talent will be evident as you browse this collection of 'ukulele solos and ensembles. As a skilled Waldorf teacher, Mr. Preston has consistently provided superb student performances with his very popular 'ukulele classes and ensembles.

The melodic method of teaching 'ukulele presented in this book will enhance your goals far beyond merely introducing simple chords and sing-alongs. The 'ukulele itself is a perfect instrument for personal and group musical expression. Its price, size, and versatility will be appreciated by students and parents of all grade levels. The inclusion of a wide range of musical examples from around the world and the Pacific will be a delightful supplement to your lessons on geography and culture.

I cannot recommend this resource enough—please buy copies for all of your students and find out what great music they can make alone and with their friends. Amaze parents and friends with a fun 'ukulele ensemble that develops more advanced music reading and Hawaiian strumming skills. Challenge yourself and your students with a new way of enjoying this popular instrument.

Dr. Barbara Payne McLain
Professor of Music
University of Hawai'i, Mānoa

PREFACE

This book has grown out of a deep affection for the 'ukulele. It is easy to fall in love with an instrument so friendly and social. I remember once playing in a folk band in winter and the leader turning and saying, 'It's amazing, I can hear the sun in your 'ukulele!'

My father taught me the basics as a boy, but I was first exposed to 'kanikapila,' or the social use of 'ukulele with song and other instruments, in the islands of Vanuatu, near Fiji. I had gone to the island of Espíritu Santo in Vanuatu as a volunteer teacher. There I found many people who played 'ukulele and sang with great feeling in groups, especially at 'pau hana,' or end of the working day.

When I moved to Hawai'i, many years later, I was overjoyed to find the 'ukulele as a very important instrument in most Hawaiian bands. For several years, I went almost every Friday night to Sea Life Park, where many of the Hawaiian masters played: Eddie Kamae and The Sons of Hawai'i, Israel Kamakawiwa'ole and The Makaha Sons of Ni'ihau, Dennis Pavao, Moe Keale, Jerry Santos and Haunani Apoliana of Olomana, and the duo The Ka'u Crater Boys with the amazing 'ukulele player Troy Fernandez. I later took some lessons from Troy and continue to admire his flawless sense of rhythm and what he did to bring fresh fire to the heart of 'ukulele playing. Roy Sakuma, too, has been a great inspiration.

After fifteen years of taking lessons and teaching elementary to intermediate 'ukulele to children and adults, I wanted to bring together my method and some of my material in book form.

I found many friends and professional musicians here in Hawai'i who were very encouraging of the idea of a 'ukulele book such as I had in mind, with a step-by-step method, teaching sight-reading and chords, and with a CD with examples to listen to and play along with!

I am extraordinarily grateful to Bennett Hymer and the team at Mutual Publishing for supporting me in the writing of this book, and to the aloha of Hawai'i and its people for many years of music, inspiration, and kindness.

Michael Preston

ACKNOWLEDGMENTS

Warmest thanks are owed to many different people who supported the idea and the practical realization of this approach to learning 'ukulele.

In particular:

The Honolulu Waldorf School for its great generosity in making possible, through my sabbatical, the time to write this book and its support of its 'ukulele program over many years.

Frederick Kamaka Jr. and the Kamaka family of Kamaka Hawai'i, Inc. for their aloha in granting access to and photography of their 'ukulele and the photograph of the founder, Samuel Kamaka.

Ray Wong of Pacific Light Studios for the skillful photography of modeled 'ukulele skills throughout the book.

Kaz Tanabe for his photography of the Kamaka 'ukulele in the introduction.

Bryan Kessler and Steve Jones of Wire and Wood Studios for their enthusiasm and professionalism in recording the CD for the book.

Sharde Pratt for her aloha, mana, and beauty as the model for this book.

Leolani Pratt, kumu hula, for her friendship and support and her advice about anything and everything Hawaiian over fifteen years.

Dr. Barbara McLain for her ready support and professional advice in all matters musical!

My son Joseph Preston for his skilled help in computer graphics and the drawing for stringing the 'ukulele.

Nathan Mata, who teaches 'ukulele at schools and at his studio, Akamai Music and Enrichment, for his helpful input and encouragement.

Herb Ota for his comments and support.

Ron Chun for his interest in and warmth toward the project, and for his great aloha in playing bass for different 'ukulele groups at school concerts over the years.

The memory of Eddie Bush, a very fine 'ukulele player, gentleman, and wise friend and colleague.

The memory of Les Reitfors, who made the most exquisite 'ukulele and gave me my 'ukulele, one of his early models. He was a warmhearted and truly wonderful craftsman!

All the children and adult students I have worked with. Special mahalo to the members of the Pua Nani Players: Briana Anderson, Oriana Blanco, Rachel Haymer, Ashley Reitfors, and Sophia Sydow for their musicality and joy in informal kanikapila and their many public performances. Also to Jana Pintz and Dylan Nash, original members.

Last but not least, my wife Tanya, for her love, support, and great patience!

Many thanks to the following for kind permission to use their material:

Kahauanu Lake for permission to use his beautiful song *Pua Lililehua*.

The Hal Leonard Corporation for permission to include *Jamaica Farewell*.

Nalu Music for permission to use the picture of the Hawaiian musicians in the introduction.

Axel Richter, who has written a 'ukulele handbook on tunings and chords, for his permission to use the photograph of the braguinha. Axel's website: www.folk-axel.de

INTRODUCTION

• This book will teach you how to play the most frequently used chords and keys along with many rhythms, including Hawaiian roll and triplet strums.

• If you want to go further, this book will also show you how to pick melodies, including the use of tremolo.

The 'ukulele has become one of the most popular instruments in the last ten years. It is a light, portable, and easy-to-use strum accompaniment to 'kanikapila,' or to play along with others on the lānai or at a party.

But the 'ukulele can also play melodies, often mixed with chords. At this level, it can be a lead instrument for serious performance.

Many people are happy just to learn chords and some strumming rhythms so they can accompany themselves and others in singing. Among the sweetest qualities of the 'ukulele are its friendliness, its sunny sound, and the ease with which you can learn to play it this way!

Most Hawaiian musicians learn 'by ear.' But to do this you have to be taught by a musician and copy his or her techniques. Sometimes this can be very expensive and once you don't have the musician's help, you cannot progress.

If you do not have a teacher and want to teach yourself, this book will show you how to strum chords and play melodies.

You can listen to the CD and hear how each example is played.

Once you have begun to master sight-reading and chords, you will be able to play many kinds of music, such as folk, pop, international, and classical.

To enjoy learning, you need a mix of easy skills and fun of strumming along to songs with the slower but lifelong skill of playing melody as well.

You can learn from this book in two ways:
1. Study strumming and accompaniment skills only and skip the sight-reading.
2. Study lesson by lesson, learning strumming and melody skills.

Either way, you will find a true friend in your 'ukulele—a companion to relax you and give you joy and to enable you to make music alone or with others!

LET'S KANIKAPILA!

ABOUT THE 'UKULELE

CHOOSING A 'UKULELE
Most 'ukulele players start on a small 'ukulele called a soprano or standard 'ukulele.

Often your first 'ukulele is a simple one. As you get better at playing, you will feel the need for a better 'ukulele. How to know what is the best match for you?

To find the right 'ukulele you first need to know a bit about the history of the 'ukulele and the modern types that are for sale.

A BRIEF HISTORY
Portuguese travelers to Hawai'i are credited with bringing to Hawai'i the ancestor of the modern 'ukulele. In Portugal and the Madeira Islands there were two commonly used instruments shaped like guitars but smaller and with only four strings. One was the cavaquinho and the other the braguinha.

ARRIVAL IN HAWAI'I
In August 1879, over four hundred Portuguese immigrants arrived in Honolulu harbor. Aboard the ship were five musicians and musical craftsmen. Legend has it that at the moment of docking, one of them, João Fernandes, borrowed a braguinha and with others began playing and singing Portuguese music in gratitude for a safe arrival. Hawaiians fell in love with the little instrument, naming it the "ukulele'.

Braguinha

THE FIRST 'UKULELE
Some say the 'ukulele was named "uku' (flea) and 'lele' (jumping) because the quick movements of the instrumentalist reminded them of this.

Others say the name came from Queen Lili'uokalani, the word 'uku' meaning gift and 'lele' meaning to come—the gift that arrived.

Yet others say the name comes from "ūkēkē lele' or 'dancing 'ūkēkē' (the 'ūkēkē is a Hawaiian musical bow).

Whatever the source, the name stuck and the melodic sound of the name has a happy ring to it.

Manuel Nunes, one of the musicians, opened up a shop in Honolulu to make and sell 'ukulele. Records show that by 1884, Nunes and Augusto Dias had both opened 'ukulele businesses.

 About the 'Ukulele

Within a short time, the instrument found its way to the court of King David Kalākaua, Hawai'i's 'Merrie Monarch.' King Kalākaua, a fine guitarist, welcomed the 'ukulele as an accompaniment to hula.

The first 'ukulele made by Diaz, Santo, and Manuel Nunes became much sought after by Hawaiian royalty. Musicians and visitors to the islands usually wanted to take one back as a special memento of Hawai'i.

1892—The 'ukulele becomes part of local life.

Samuel Kamaka

HAWAI'I'S BEST-KNOWN MAKER OF FINE 'UKULELE

In 1916, Hawai'i's best-known 'ukulele maker, Samuel Kamaka, apprenticed himself to Manuel Nunes. The family business expanded steadily and to this day is the principal and best-known manufacturer of fine koa 'ukulele.

Probably the majority of Hawaiian musicians can be seen playing Kamakas. They are distinctive for being made of well-cured koa, having a clear tone, having superior tuning keys, staying in tune, being very dependable, and always looking good!

Another top-quality 'ukulele is made by Martin. Martin 'ukulele are much sought after for their beautiful tone, but they are made outside of Hawai'i and are not usually made of koa, Hawai'i's most distinctive and beautiful wood.

Because of the resurgence of interest in 'ukulele, there are other very good makers on the market. Some recent 'ukulele look more beautiful than either Kamakas or Martins. For display purposes they might be preferable, but for a musician, looks alone are not enough!

The following are five main styles of 'ukulele regardless of maker. Each is preferred by musicians for different reasons. You will begin to be able to judge which style might be a match for your skills and needs.

Standard or soprano 'ukulele

Standard or Soprano 'Ukulele

This is the most common size. All four strings are nylon. It is strung G (above middle C), C, E, and A. It has a bright, high sound.

The whole soprano, from tip of neck to end of sound box is about 21 inches in length. Vibrating string length is up to 14 inches long. This is the more accurate way to determine size. Vibrating string length is the length of the string from the nut, where the fingerboard begins, to the bridge.

Concert 'ukulele

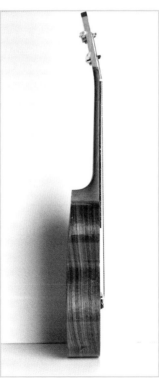

Concert 'ukulele, side view

Concert 'Ukulele

The concert is a little longer. The total length is about 23 inches. The string length is between 14½ and 16 inches.

The sound box is usually a bit bigger for more volume and sometimes rounded for better tone. Nylon strings are used but many players put a wound string on the G to drop it an octave. Sometimes the C string is the wound string. This gives the 'ukulele a richer, fuller sound.

As the fingerboard is longer, there is a little more space to place the fingers. If you have big hands, you should consider this as the minimum size.

Tenor 'Ukulele

The tenor 'ukulele is approximately 26 inches long. Like the concert 'ukulele, it has more frets than the soprano, enabling one to play a higher melody line. The string length is usually 17 to 18 inches.

The tenor is the preferred model of many professional musicians for two reasons:
1. The neck is noticeably longer, giving more room for the left hand.
2. The sound production is louder, with richer deep notes and a mellow tone overall.

Six-String 'Ukulele

The six-string or Lili'u tenor-sized 'ukulele is very popular as an accompanying instrument for performance and hula. The first or highest A string is doubled with a wound string an octave lower. The third or C string is paired with a second one. With the 'octaved' first string carrying the highest and therefore 'lead' note of each chord, the clarity and emphasis are heightened.

Tenor 'ukulele

Playing this as a melody instrument is not so comfortable, as the slightest difference in tuning between the two top strings will spoil the melody line. The more strings you have on an instrument, the more tension there is, and so pressing down—or 'action,' as it is called—is harder. On the other hand, the volume is greater!

Six-string 'ukulele

Eight-String 'Ukulele

The eight-string is also a tenor-sized 'ukulele but strengthened to take the tension of double the number of strings. It is therefore heavier and harder to keep in tune. Its strings are tuned in the following way: The two top strings (A and E) are doubled.

The two lower strings (C and G) each have a high and a low octave.

Many singers for hula groups use this model for the volume and richness of the chords. With the distinctive roll and triplet strums of Hawaiian dance music, the eight-string 'ukulele is warm, rich, and authoritative in its sound. It is not, however, recommended as a novice's instrument.

Eight-string 'ukulele

Now that you have a picture of the styles available, you can decide on the right 'ukulele for your needs. Price is a big factor. Top models, like the Kamaka models below, sell for upward of $800!

At the other end of the scale, you can buy a decent standard for about $150. It is possible to buy a new 'ukulele for under $100, but be aware that it is likely to either develop problems or suffer in tone. On the other hand, you can pick up a secondhand 'ukulele from an ad in the paper that can sometimes be worth double its price.

There is one other approach: Start with a cheap, 'tourist' 'ukulele. When you know you want a 'long-term relationship' with a 'ukulele, then get someone's help and go shop carefully for a good one, one that will become your best friend.

The five main members of the 'ukulele family, from left to right: standard or soprano 'ukulele, concert 'ukulele, tenor 'ukulele, six-string 'ukulele, and eight-string 'ukulele.

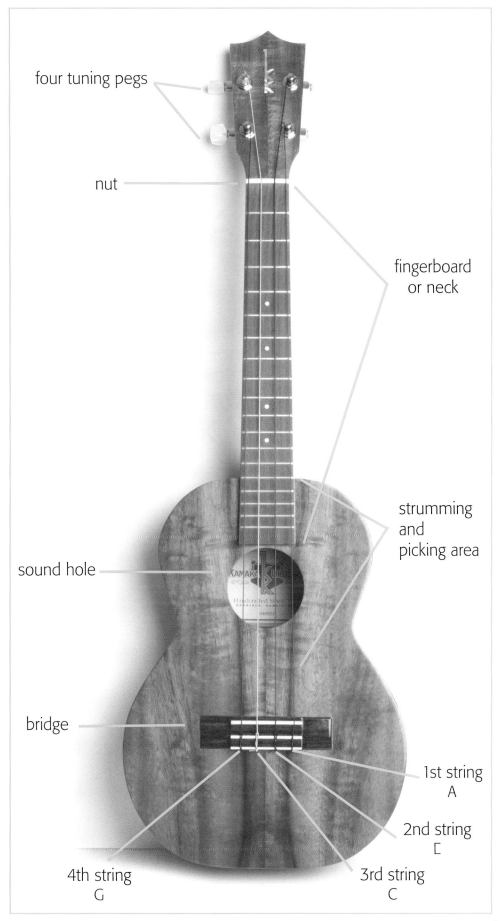

four tuning pegs

nut

fingerboard
or neck

strumming
and
picking area

sound hole

bridge

1st string
A

2nd string
E

4th string
G

3rd string
C

The 'ukulele is tuned to particular intervals so that the chord patterns work. If you are playing alone you can actually drop or raise the entire tuning to suit your needs. However, for sight-reading and playing along with other instruments, this is the common tuning:

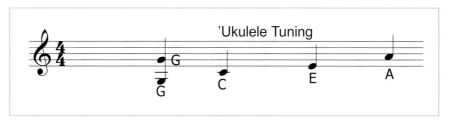

Many 'ukulele players put a wound string on G to get a richer chord sound and so they can play a melody deeper, below middle C. This is why you see two G notes above. The higher G is usual on the soprano and concert models.

To get the right notes, use a tuning pipe or just take your notes from a piano, a keyboard, or even a wooden flute. Learn the 'melody' of these notes so that, in time, you will only need the starting note and can tune up without a pipe or other instrument. A good ukulele will keep in tune once the strings have 'settled down.'

A. Slotted Bridges: Knot the string and pull it tight into the correct slot.

B. Peg Bridges: A few 'ukulele have pegs. Knot the string
    and 'peg' it into the correct hole.

C. Bridges with holes:

    1.   Pass the correct string through the correct hole in the bridge.
    2.   Bring the string back to loop around itself.
    3   Wind the string around itself at least twice.
    4.   Trim to leave about 1/4 inch extending. Wind other end on peg and pull tight.

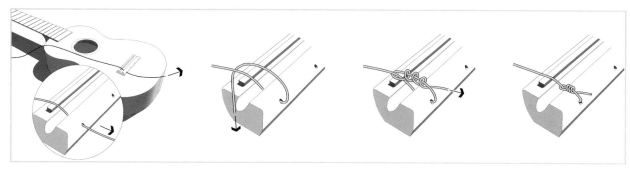

Stringing a 'ukulele

A new string will always stretch. You can speed up stability by pre-stretching:

    1.   Tighten to the correct pitch.
    2.   Gently stretch by lifting the string about an inch above the fingerboard and flexing it up and down a few times.
    3.   Re-tension to the correct pitch. Repeat these steps until, when you stretch the string, it stays in tune or very nearly in tune. You will probably have to retune a new string for the next two or three times you take out the 'ukulele to play. By then the strings should settle down and stay in tune.

THE PATTERN OF EACH LESSON

1. Chord Practice

At the beginning of each lesson there will be a chord practice section. This teaches you new chords in a sequence that makes the playing enjoyable.

The exercises take you from lots of strums to one strum a chord before playing the second one, then the third, then the fourth.

Each practice sequence uses the same chords again but reduces the number of strums so that you have to change more quickly.

When you really have them down, you can change each chord after only one strum!

2. Strumming to Melodies

The next section has you use your new chords in simple melodies. As you progress you will know more and more chords. You can listen to the CD to hear the suggested strumming rhythm for the particular melody.

3. Learning the Notes

In the third section you will learn two or three new notes each lesson. There are diagrams to help you and you can listen to the exercises on the CD. This part needs the most concentration.

4. Playing the Melodies

The last part of each lesson has you try to play a part of a scale using the new notes, followed by two or three melodies that use these new notes. As you progress, the melodies naturally get more interesting.

Progressing

As you progress, the chords become more varied and the melodies will shift into Hawaiian, Pacific, and international tunes with chord accompaniment and words.

Each step and each lesson are specially designed not to 'jump' too quickly!

At any time you can listen and follow along to the CD.

Note: Most CD players, or their remote, have a repeat button. You can have a particular track play multiple times so you can catch the exercise, rhythm, or melody.

Lesson 1

HOLDING AND STRUMMING THE 'UKULELE

The best position to hold the 'ukulele

The picture on the left shows you the best position to hold the 'ukulele. Your right forearm pins it against you, about halfway down your chest on your right.

The left hand holds the neck of the 'ukulele lightly and the hand is positioned to bring the fingers over to play notes and chords. Tuck your left elbow in, but not tightly.

Relax!

Strumming the 'ukulele

Open your right hand and let it go limp. Extend your index finger a little and with a gentle, loose up-and-down movement strum the four strings up and down with the end of your index finger (part fingernail, part pad). Your thumb should be extended parallel to the neck of the 'ukulele and be completely relaxed, spaced a little from the hand. This helps your whole hand to be fluid.

Don't try to play any chords yet. Just practice strumming: down – up – down – up – down – up – down.

Once you feel you can do this comfortably, go to the next page to learn your first three chords in the key of C. This is a very common chord family for many tunes.

PLAYING THE FIRST CHORDS

Creating harmony is one of the most enjoyable elements of music.
You will be able to accompany yourself and others with chords
on the 'ukulele very soon.

Understanding 'Ukulele Chord Pictures
When new chords are presented you will see a grid like this:

The horizontal spaces represent the frets on the 'ukulele.
The vertical lines represent the four strings.

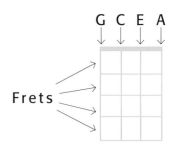

To play the simplest chord, the C chord, place your third finger down on the first (A) string, third fret. Whenever a new chord is taught you will also see a photograph showing the correct position of hand and fingers.

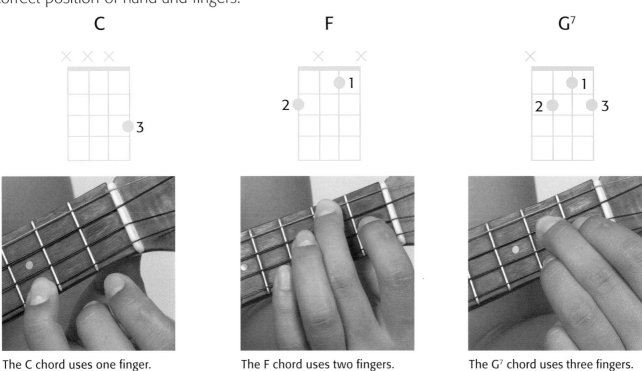

| C | F | G⁷ |

The C chord uses one finger.   The F chord uses two fingers.   The G⁷ chord uses three fingers.

For all chords and notes, the fingers
of the **left hand** are numbered this way:

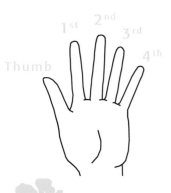

Make sure you get a clean sound. If a note sounds muffled or 'fuzzy,' it is because you are not pressing it down onto the fingerboard fully.

If this happens build the chord by putting one finger down, making sure it sounds clean, then the next and so on.

Practice will make this happen easily!

A RHYTHM APPROACH TO LEARNING CHORDS QUICKLY: THE SEQUENCES

Using six different rhythms you will progress from strumming each chord **EIGHT** times to eventually strumming each chord only **ONCE** before changing to the next chord!
This approach gives the brain lots of time to absorb the finger pattern and retain it as 'finger memory.' If you can make clean chord changes every two strums (march rhythm), you are really close to mastery!

First Exercise: Eight Beats  CD track 1

Strum each chord eight times before moving to next chord

8 x	then	8 x	then	8 x	then	8 x
C		F		G⁷		C

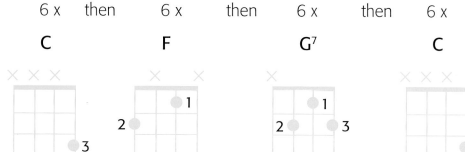

Second Exercise: Six Beats (double waltz rhythm)  CD track 2

Strum each chord six times before moving to next chord

6 x	then	6 x	then	6 x	then	6 x
C		F		G⁷		C

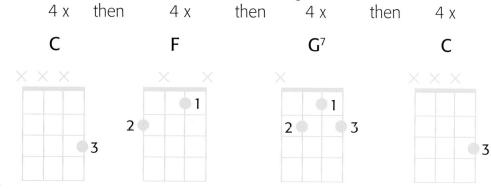

Third Exercise: Four Beats (pop or jazz rhythm) CD track 3

Strum each chord four times before moving to next chord

4 x	then	4 x	then	4 x	then	4 x
C		F		G⁷		C

Fourth Exercise: Three Beats (waltz rhythm) 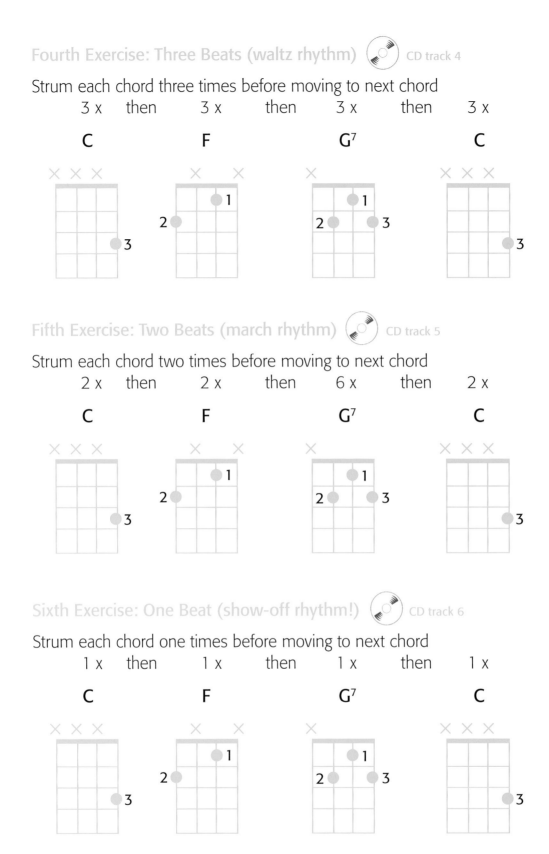 CD track 4

Strum each chord three times before moving to next chord

3 x   then   3 x   then   3 x   then   3 x

C   F   G⁷   C

Fifth Exercise: Two Beats (march rhythm) CD track 5

Strum each chord two times before moving to next chord

2 x   then   2 x   then   6 x   then   2 x

C   F   G⁷   C

Sixth Exercise: One Beat (show-off rhythm!) CD track 6

Strum each chord one times before moving to next chord

1 x   then   1 x   then   1 x   then   1 x

C   F   G⁷   C

In each lesson a new chord family will be introduced.
Use these sequences with the new chords to practice.

14   Lesson 1

Now try your skills at strumming accompaniment for this tune
with a steady four beats—four down—strums per measure or bar.  CD track 7

SKIP TO MY LOU

Traditional

STRUMMING IS LIKE ONE-HAND DRUMMING

Good strumming is built on a sense of rhythm. If you can tap out the rhythm of a tune with your foot or hand, you have the core of what is needed. The difference is that with a 'ukulele you create percussion not only downward but also upward, as your hand comes up.

As you go through the lessons, you will learn different strum rhythms. But in this lesson, as you are new to the chords, just go on instinct. You can try a rhythm before playing the tune with the chords by damping—very lightly covering all the strings with your left hand and just strumming up and down to hear how the rhythm sounds.

Keep your right hand very relaxed! Let your own feeling for the strumming up and down guide you. Strum up and down slowly and then pick up speed.

When you feel satisfied, listen to the CD and strum along to the tune. Keep the beat but do not worry if your rhythm is not an exact copy of what you hear. It is up to an individual player's artistry to make variations.

No two players keeping the same beat will strum identically.  CD track 8

WHEN THE SAINTS COME MARCHING IN

African-American folk song

Lesson 1

PICKING MELODY: THE FIRST THREE NOTES—C, D, AND E

Here are the first three notes.

When the string is played **without any fingers** down it is called **open**. It has a **0** to show that no finger should be down. Otherwise there are only four possible fingers you will use to create notes for melody.

At the beginning, you will use only the second finger.

$\boxed{0}$ = no finger down $\boxed{2}$ = 2nd finger down

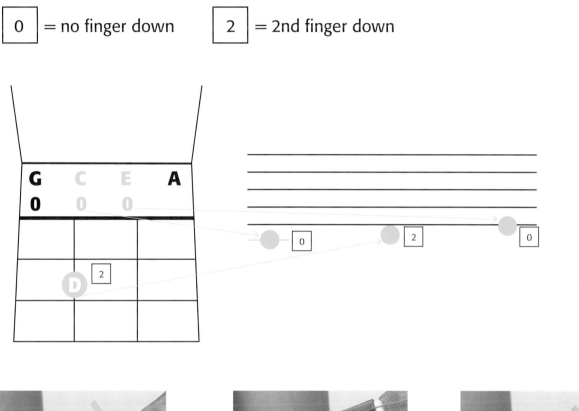

C—no finger

D—2nd finger

E—no finger

Once you have studied the diagram and the photos,
try the first exercise on the next page, playing up and down the three notes.

In the music below you will see:
Above each note is the **finger number**, below each note is its **name**.  CD track 9

FIRST EXERCISE USING C, D, AND E

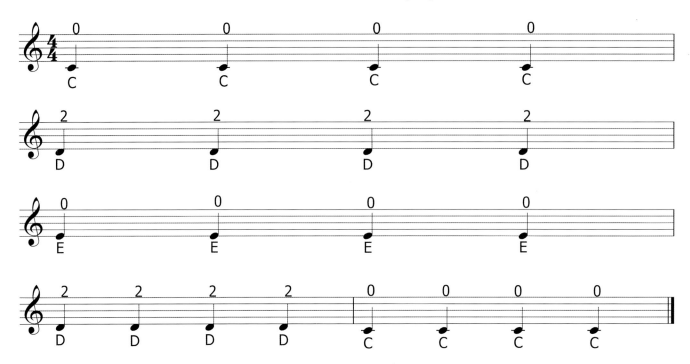

NOW TRY YOUR FIRST MELODY: *HOT CROSS BUNS*

If you have never read regular music notation before, this simple, two- or three-note introduction to each lesson will teach you, in easy steps, the names and positions of each note on the stave (the five horizontal lines) as you need them, going through the lessons.

You will learn to sight-read much quicker if you also sing the names of the notes as you play them. Research shows that if several senses are engaged at once, we memorize things quicker. You will be looking at the note, playing it with your fingers, and also naming it using speech and hearing.

1. Start very slowly. Repeat the passage slowly. Then try slightly quicker. CD track 10

HOT CROSS BUNS

2. Now try *Hot Cross Buns* in double time—listen to the CD first.  CD track 11

3. Try *Hot Cross Buns* in waltz time. Notice the time signature on the left.
It is 3/4. Notice the fingering numbers and letters have been left out.
Hopefully you can now manage! Listen to the CD to hear how it goes first. CD track 12

 The original tune is in 4/4, meaning that in each bar there are four beats—shown by the upper number.

Waltz time has three beats to each bar—shown by the upper number.

The lower number means what kind of notes the melody is set in—eighth, quarter, or half notes.

Lesson 2

DOWN-UP STRUMMING

We will begin practicing down-up strumming. It will add life and swing to your playing.

In Lesson One, you practiced chords with six different types of beat. However, you used a **single down-strum** for each beat; you strummed **down** eight times, six times, four times, and so on for each chord. (Each ↓ is a down-strum.)

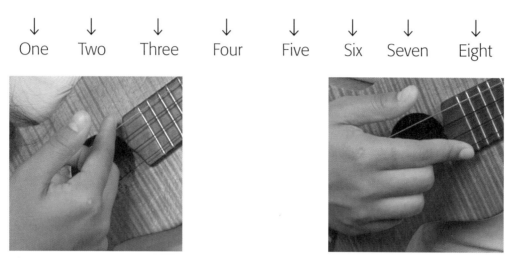

↓	↓	↓	↓	↓	↓	↓	↓
One	Two	Three	Four	Five	Six	Seven	Eight

Picture 1: Down-strum   Picture 2: Up-strum

Strum down with the right-hand edge of your index finger (looking at the back of the hand), using the pad and a little bit of the fingernail.

Strum up with the soft pad of your finger. Your finger does not stay straight but relaxes in a curve as it rises up, to end up in the down-strum position in Picture 1.

Now we will add an **up-strum** to the same exercise.
This means you will keep the same beat but actually double the amount of strums. (Each ↑ is an up-strum.)

On ↓ strum down and count a number. On ↑ strum up and say 'and.'

↓   ↑   ↓   ↑   ↓   ↑   ↓   ↑   ↓   ↑   ↓   ↑   ↓   ↑   ↓   ↑
One-and-**Two**-and-**Three**-and-**Four**-and-**Five**-and-**Six**-and-**Seven**-and-**Eight**-and-

Now try the sequence (see pages 13 and 14) in the new way, always counting as you strum, to keep your beat steady!

(see pages 13 and 14)

First Exercise: Eight Beats with an **up-strum** between each beat  CD track 13

Listen to the CD to hear how it should sound. You can get faster later.

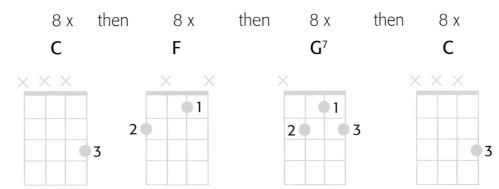

8 x	then	8 x	then	8 x	then	8 x
C		F		G⁷		C

Second Exercise: Six Beats (stress the first of each three beats) CD track 14

Third Exercise: Four Beats CD track 15

Fourth Exercise: Three Beats (stress the first of each three beats)  CD track 15

Fifth Exercise: Two Beats CD track 15

Sixth Exercise: One Beat CD track 15

TRYING OUT THE DOWN-UP STRUM

Now that you have begun to feel relaxed in your down-up strumming, try the well-known tune *Swanee River.* This can be played throughout with a simple and relaxed down-up strum.

 CD track 16

SWANEE RIVER

Stephen Foster

Way down u-pon the Swa-nee Ri-ver, Far, far a-way,
All up and down the whole cre-a-tion Sad-ly I roam,

That's where my heart is turn-ing e-ver, That's where the old folks — stay.
Still long-ing for the old plan-ta-tion And for the old folks at home.

All the world is sad and drear-y ev-'ry where I roam.

O, bro-thers, how my heart grows wear-y, Far from the old folks at home.

On the next page, continue to practice your chords and the down-up strum in the Australian tune *Kookaburra.*

 CD track 17

KOOKABURRA

Koo - ka - bur - ra sits on the old gum tree, ——

Mer - ry, mer - ry king of the bush is he. ——

Laugh, koo - ka - bur - ra, laugh, koo - ka - bur - ra,

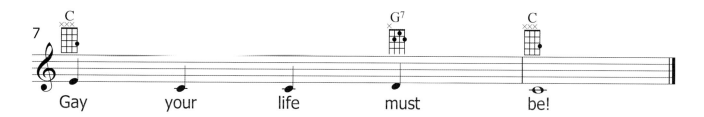

Gay your life must be!

NOW TRY *OH, SUSANNA!*

This will involve a mixture of down-strums with an up-strum between.
Here is the pattern:

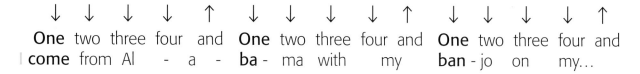

↓ ↓ ↓ ↓ ↑ ↓ ↓ ↓ ↓ ↑ ↓ ↓ ↓ ↓ ↑
One two three four and **One** two three four and **One** two three four and
I **come** from Al - a - **ba** - ma with my **ban** - jo on my…

Pick-up/Lead-in

Notice at the beginning of the tune, and again at bar 5 (see page 24), there are lead-ins, i.e., **I**- and **I'm**-. These lead-in notes are officially called pick-up notes. Pick-up notes make the up-beat, which leads into the down-beat of the following full bar.

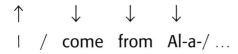

STRUMMING AND COUNTING

To start the tune you can count **ONE TWO THREE FOUR** (to set the speed) then
ONE TWO THREE to lead in, with the pick-up on the fourth or final beat before the next bar:

↑	↓	↓	↓
	/	come from	Al-a-/ …

Listen to the CD to hear the rhythm.  CD track 18

OH, SUSANNA!

Stephen Foster

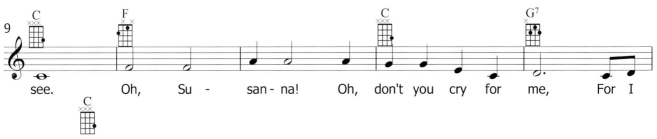

Lesson 3

INTRODUCING KEY AND CHORDS OF F

Study the fingerings for the new chords B♭ and C⁷.
Your sequence now is: F, B♭, C⁷, F, chords in the key of F.
Practice the sequence 8,6,4,3,2,1 that you used with
the key of C chords in Lessons One and Two.

CD track 19

You already know the chord of F so it is not pictured here.
Do not be discouraged by the B♭ chord. This is one of the hardest chords to get a clear sound from because the first finger holds down two strings: the A and the E string. It will take you some time to get used to it, but that is normal. After you use it for a while it will steadily get clearer. In compensation, the C⁷ chord is very easy!

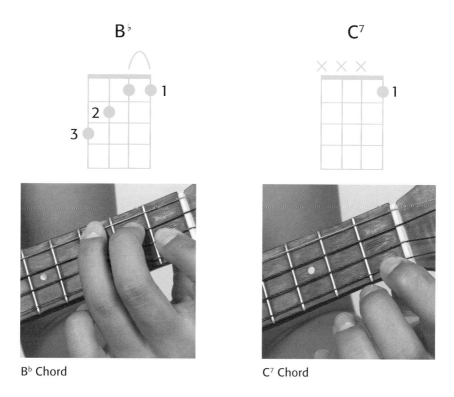

B♭ Chord   C⁷ Chord

Go back to Lesson One if you need help in remembering the sequences.
Make sure you go through this sequence twice!

Before going on to new music,
note these teaching points to prepare for further sight-reading.

About Note Value

This is a whole note—worth four beats

Count:
One, Two, Three, Four

This is a half note—worth two beats

Count:
One, Two   Three, Four

This is a quarter note—worth one beat

Count:
One   Two   Three   Four

These are eighth notes—worth half a beat each

Count:
One   and   Two   and   Three   and   Four   and

Key Signatures

A **key signature** is shown at the beginning of each line of music (called a system).
Once you know what key a piece of music is in, you will know which chord family to use and also you will be able to start on the right note (pitch a song correctly).

There are many possible keys in music, some very difficult to play.
In this book we will study the most common and important keys for the 'ukulele.

Below are the two keys introduced so far: **the key of C and the key of F.**

F is one of the most popular keys for Hawaiian music, as it is at a good level for singing and it is also an easy key to pick melodies in.

The key of C is plain without any sign (accidental)

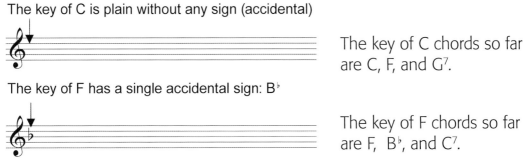

The key of F has a single accidental sign: B♭

The key of C chords so far are C, F, and G⁷.

The key of F chords so far are F, B♭, and C⁷.

Try the new chords in this well-known folk song.  CD track 20

RED RIVER VALLEY

Traditional

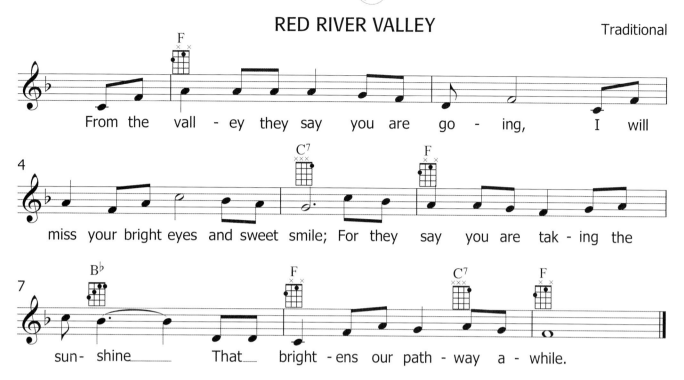

From the vall - ey they say you are go - ing, I will
miss your bright eyes and sweet smile; For they say you are tak - ing the
sun- shine____ That__ bright - ens our path - way a - while.

Try accompanying the next song with chords before studying new notes to pick.  CD track 21

AULD LANG SYNE

Scottish Traditional

Should auld ac - quaint-ance be for - got and nev - er brought to
mind? Should auld ac - quaint-ance be for - got and days of Auld Lang
Syne? For Auld__ Lang__ Syne, my dear, for Auld____ Lang_ Syne, We'll
take a cup o' kind - ness yet for the sake of Auld Lang Syne.

PICKING MELODY: THREE NEW NOTES—F, G, AND A

F and G, the first two notes, lie on the E string.

F—Put your first finger down on the first fret of the E string.

G—Put the third finger down.
   (Do not use the second finger because it will play the note between F and G, called F#.
   We will be coming to that later.)

A—No finger down, an open string.

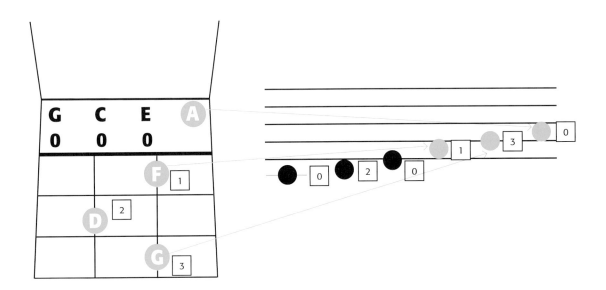

F—1st finger

G—3rd finger

A—no finger

On this page you will add the three new notes to your repertoire, bringing you one step away from a full scale. This opens up a greater range of tunes you can sight-read.

Remember, the first three steps of sight-reading present the steepest learning curve. After the third step, you will be reinforcing everything you have learned every time you play a new melody.

Later, we will be adding extra notes to enable to play in different keys and to go up higher, but the main work is in your first three steps.  CD track 22

EXERCISES ON USING F, G, AND A

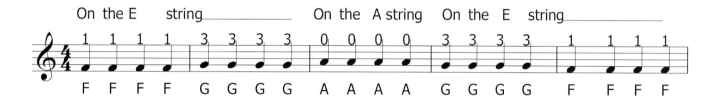

Now try exactly the same exercise in 3/4, waltz time

Revision from Lesson One

In waltz time, play the scale from C to A and back

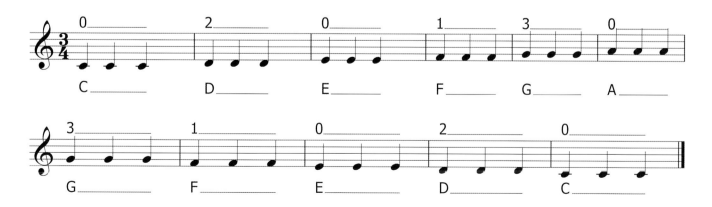

 CD track 23

TWINKLE, TWINKLE, LITTLE STAR

Now try this tune without note names
but still with the help of fingering numbers.  CD track 24

LIGHTLY ROW

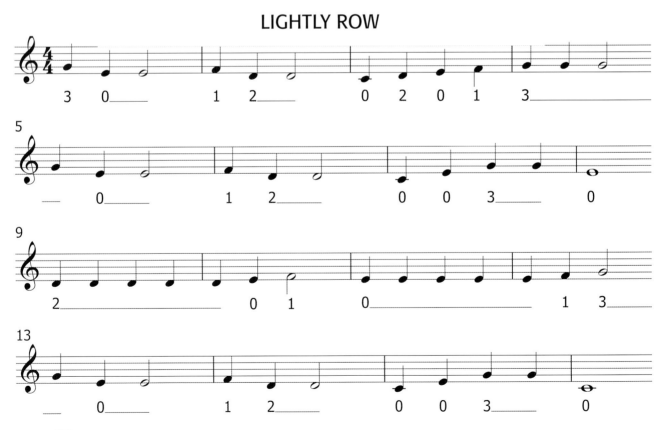

COMPLETING LESSON THREE: *DRINK TO ME ONLY WITH THINE EYES*

Notice the lines and numbers (1. and 2.) above the words 'mine' and 'wine.'
You will only see these 1st time and 2nd time symbols when a tune **repeats** the first part, as it does here. Usually, when you come back to the same point the second time through, you skip the measure under the 1. and go straight to the measure under the 2. In this case, you play both 1. and 2. as an extra-long C, which lasts six beats the first time, and five beats on the second-time repeat. This leads you into the second half of the melody.

DRINK TO ME ONLY WITH THINE EYES

CD track 25

Ben Johnson

English Traditional

Lesson 4

INTRODUCING MINOR CHORDS

So far, the simplest chords in two basic keys—C and F—have been introduced.

There are literally hundreds of chords in the 'ukulele vocabulary and you can go on adding to your repertoire for years. However, each chord family has certain very basic members that you should know and need to be able to play to accompany a tune well.

Each major or sunny-sounding chord—for example, C, F, or B♭—has its sadder-sounding twin. Each **major key** also has its related **minor key**.

The key of C (no accidentals) is, at the same time, the key of A minor.

You can find any key's minor by just counting down three from the key note.
Down three from C is C, B, and A, so its relative minor is A minor.
Down three from F is F, E, and D, so its relative minor is D minor.

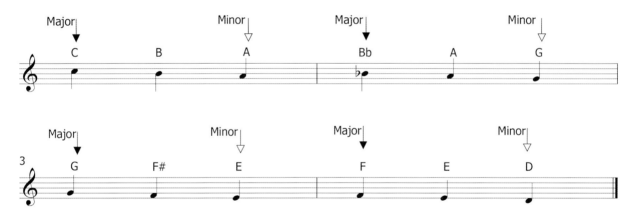

The key of C and its relative minor, A minor, have no accidentals.

When you see the key of F, it also means it is the key of D minor.
The key of F has a single accidental, B♭. It is also the key of D minor.

Below is the sequence for the key of A minor, the relative minor to the key of C major.

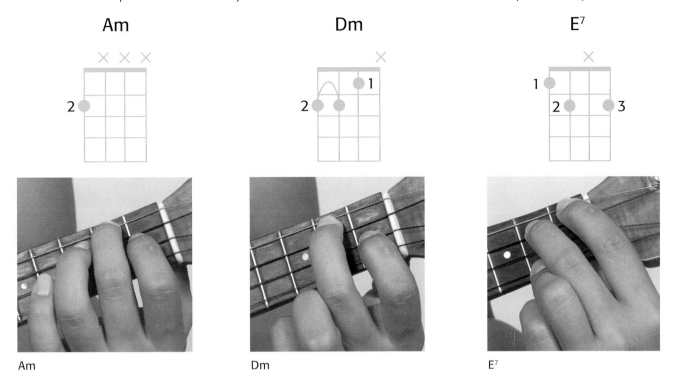

| Am | Dm | E⁷ |

Am Dm E⁷

Practice the new chord sequence using the same step system from pages 13 and 14.
Do this exercise twice. Use only your thumb and create soft down-strokes. This creates a peaceful mood, suitable for a song like *Sakura* on page 34.
Listen to the CD and follow along when you feel ready. CD track 26

Now try these chords in the beautiful song *Sakura* from Japan.  CD track 27

Again, strum with just the thumb in soft down-strokes.

SAKURA

Japanese Traditional

Slowly, peacefully

Lesson 4

COMPLETING THE C SCALE: THE LAST TWO NOTES—B AND C

The final two notes on the C scale are B and C.
B is played on the second fret of the A string with the second finger.
C is played on the third fret with the third finger.

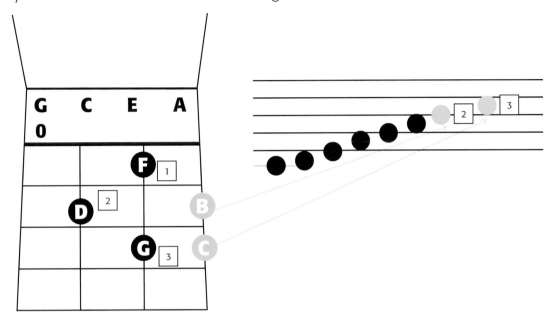

B—2nd finger, 2nd fret

C—3rd finger, 3rd fret

Try the first exercise playing just A, B, and C. CD track 28

EXERCISE USING A, B, AND C

Play in 4/4 time

Play in 3/4, waltz time

Now practice the new notes as part of the whole C scale
To help you, all note names and finger numbers are shown.  CD track 29

SCALE OF C

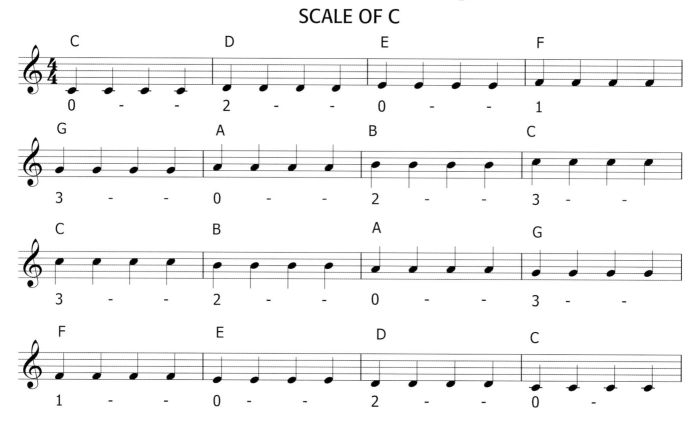

Try the next exercise without any numbering or names.
If you get stuck, go back to the first exercise.  CD track 30

SCALE OF C IN WALTZ TIME

Now try to play without fingerings or note names in waltz time.

Notice that you start on the pick-up note of E.
This means you count three and then start with the E, which is the fourth or last beat of this bar. A **bar** is also called a **measure**.

E

Notice also that there are dotted notes, such as the two Ds on the first line.

A dot after a note means that you count the value of the note plus half of itself. The Ds are scored as notes that are worth two beats, but they are also dotted. This means they are now counted as **three beats**. You will hear the note values in the CD track.

To help you, some but not all notes and fingerings have been added. This is a gentle way to help you to become independent of reminders of a note name and the finger to be used.

Try your hand at this well-known song.  CD track 31

CAMPTOWN RACES

Stephen Foster

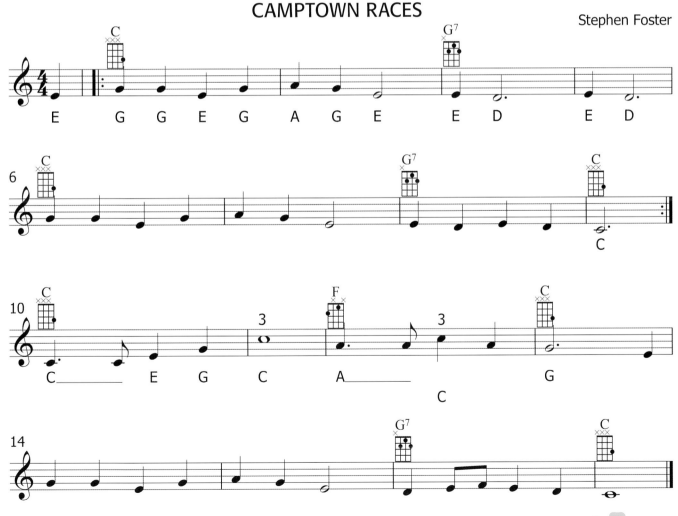

If you have become comfortable with picking all of these notes,
finish off this lesson with another Stephen Foster song *Oh, Susanna!*

Notice that in this song there are dotted quarter notes, such as
the second G in the second measure above 'Al-' and the C in the third measure above 'with.'

We played this song in Lesson Two, but only the chords. Now try to pick it.

Play along with the CD when you feel ready! CD track 32

OH, SUSANNA!

Stephen Foster

I ___ come from Al - a - bam - a with my ban - jo on my

knee. I'm going to Loui - si - an - a, My _____ true love for to

see. Oh, Su - san - na! Oh, don't you cry for me, For I

come from Al - a- bam - a with my ban - jo on my knee.

Lesson 5

CHORDS IN THE KEY OF D MINOR

Below is the sequence for the key of D minor, the relative minor to the key of F major.

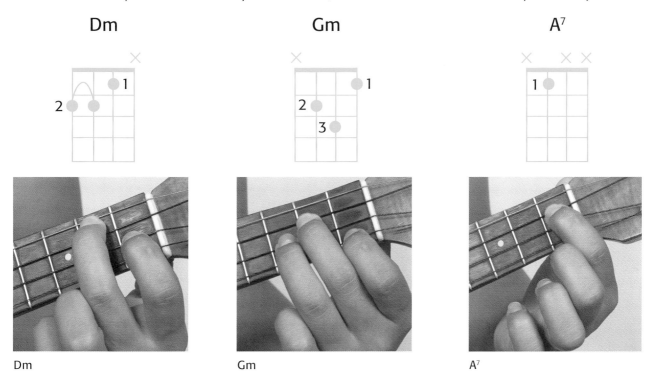

Dm   Gm   A⁷

Strum these new chords in the same sequence you have used in each lesson: Eight strums each, then six, four, and so on. Always end with the chord of Dm.

For the eight and four sequences practice adding an up-strum on the fourth beat like this:

One, Two, Three, Four -and/   One, Two, Three, Four -and/   One, Two, Three, Four -and

Erie Canal has this type of rhythm, so use it when you play the song.

Strum along with the following tune, use the rhythm introduced on page 39.  CD track 33

FINGER-PICKING CHORDS

The 'ukulele, often thought of as a strumming instrument, can be the sweetest and most charming accompanist to singing or other instruments when the chords are picked in a rhythmic pattern. This is known as chord finger-picking.

There are many patterns. Once you get comfortable with some basic ones you can make up your own.

To start, the simplest pattern in 4/4 time is given.

In order to do this effectively use your **thumb** for **down-strokes** and **1st (index) finger** for **up-strokes**.

Look at the pictures and diagrams on the next page to see how the sequence goes.

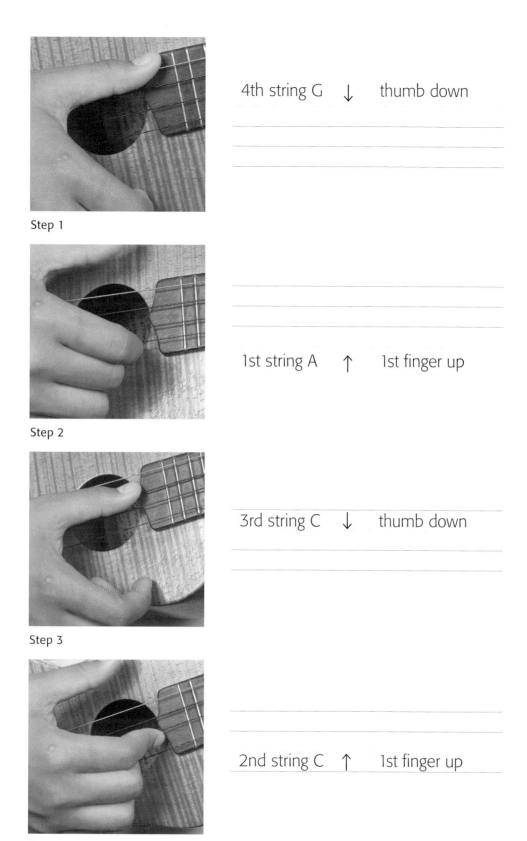

4th string G ↓ thumb down

Step 1

1st string A ↑ 1st finger up

Step 2

3rd string C ↓ thumb down

Step 3

2nd string C ↑ 1st finger up

Step 4

The thumb plays the 4th and 3rd strings. Index plays the 1st and 2nd strings.
The string playing order is: 4, 1, 3, 2. The finger pattern is: thumb, 1st, thumb, 1st.

Another way to remember is: The two outer strings (top and bottom) are played first,
then the two inner (middle) ones. The thumb is always on the down-beat.

PRACTICE FINGER-PICKING A CHORD SEQUENCE

1. Take this sequence very slowly just using the open strings, no chords.  CD track 34

2. Slowly get quicker until you feel you do not need to think and your fingers have taken over.

3. Now transfer this skill to your first and most familiar chord sequence: C, F, G⁷, C.

To do this, count in 4/4 time for each chord before changing to the next one.
Listen to the CD to hear how the sequence should go.  CD track 35

↓   ↑   ↓   ↑   ↓   ↑   ↓   ↑
One   and   Two   and   Three   and   Four   and

When you have practiced with the C–F–G⁷–C sequence, try your skill in finger-picking
with the first line of *Sakura*.

Practice the Am–Dm–E⁷–Am sequence first, with a steady count. Then try playing the song.

Remember, in your counting, 'Sa-' will have a **down-up**, 'ku-' will have a **down-up,**
and 'ra' will have **two down-ups** because it is two beats in length.

Play along with the CD to feel how it goes. CD track 36

SAKURA

Slowly, peacefully   Japanese Traditional

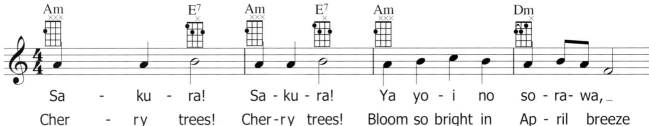

Sa - ku - ra!   Sa - ku - ra!   Ya   yo - i   no   so - ra- wa,
Cher - ry   trees!   Cher-ry trees!   Bloom so bright in   Ap - ril   breeze

Later in this lesson we will use this skill to accompany the song *Aura Lee*.

KEY OF F: B♭ INSTEAD OF B

In the key of F, the B♭ is played on the first fret with the first finger.
The C stays the same, on the third fret, played with the third finger.

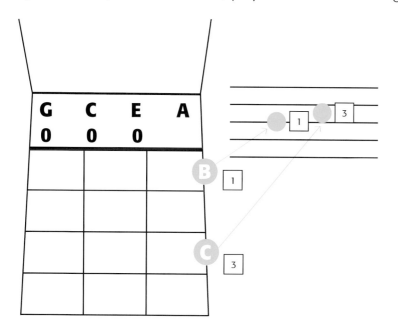

B♭

High C

The letter names except for the new note, B♭, are left out to challenge you to rely on memory.
If you forget one or two notes, go back to the scale of C, Lesson 4.
Work on this exercise. The payoff is being able to play the tunes that follow.   CD track 37

PLAYING IN THE KEY OF F

Play slowly with the CD the first time. Then try it two more times faster.

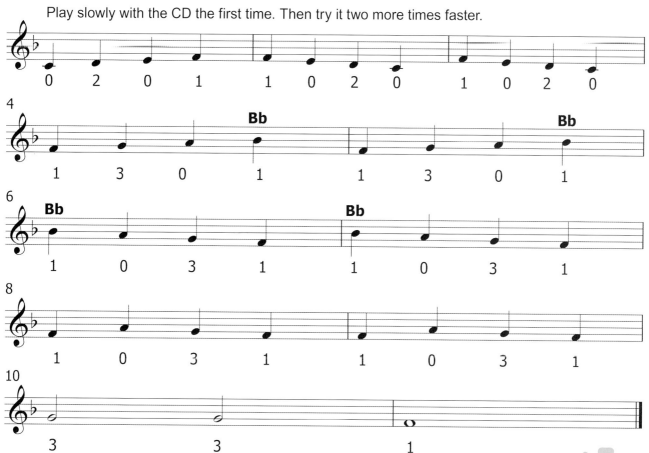

Aura Lee uses your skills in the key of F to play this classic song.
This traditional song was adapted with new lyrics by Elvis Presley as *Love Me Tender*.
The melody is also very suitable for accompaniment with the finger-picking rhythm
you have learned in this lesson. Try singing it and accompanying in this way first of all.

Then try sight-reading and picking the melody.  CD track 38

If you have someone else to play along with, switch between picking melody
to accompanying with the finger-picked chords in different verses.

Notice the repeat sign in bar 4. When you sing the second time you skip bar 4
and go directly from bar 3 to bar 5 and continue to the end.

AURA LEE

W. W. Fosdick

George R. Poulton

SIGHT-READING: *HAWAI`I PONO`Ī*

To end Lesson Five, try your hand at sight-reading *Hawai'i Pono'ī.*
This song was composed by Henry Berger, leader of the Royal Hawaiian Band
in King Kalākaua's reign. King Kalākaua added the lyrics soon after.

The song is very important in Hawai'i and all children learn it. It is sung in
state ceremonies and very often on May Day (Lei Day) in Hawai'i.

Remember that the B is a B♭ and is played on the first fret of the A string.

Listen to the CD and then try to play along when you feel ready.  CD track 39

HAWAI'I PONO'Ī

King Kalākaua   Henry Berger

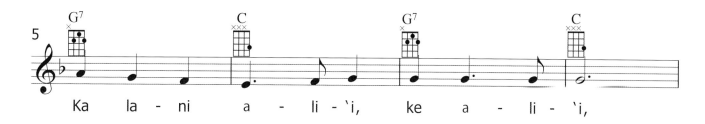

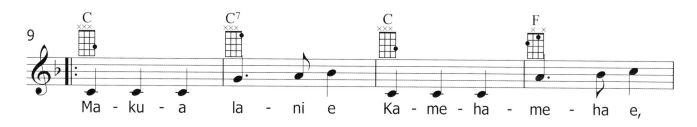

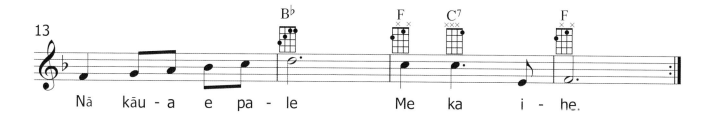

Lesson 6

CHORDS IN THE KEY OF G MAJOR

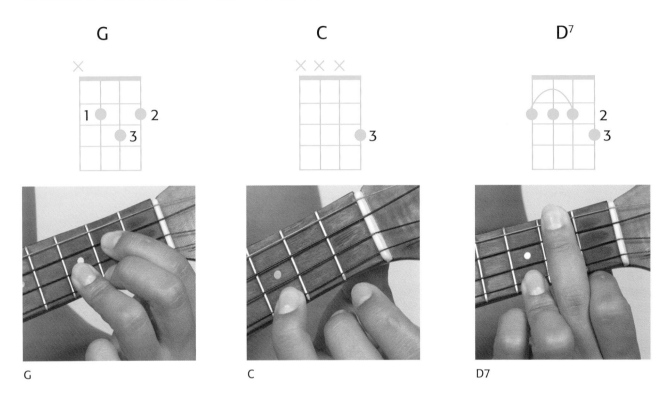

G

C

D⁷

G

C

D7

Strum these new chords in the same sequence you have used
in each lesson: Eight strums each, then six, four, and so on.

Then try **finger-picking** to the count of 8, 4, and 2 as you learned in Lesson 5.

A finger-picking rhythm for **6/4** and **3/4** time needs a different pattern.  CD track 40

Count like this:

$$\downarrow \quad \downarrow \quad \uparrow \quad \downarrow \quad \uparrow$$
One   Two   and   Three   and

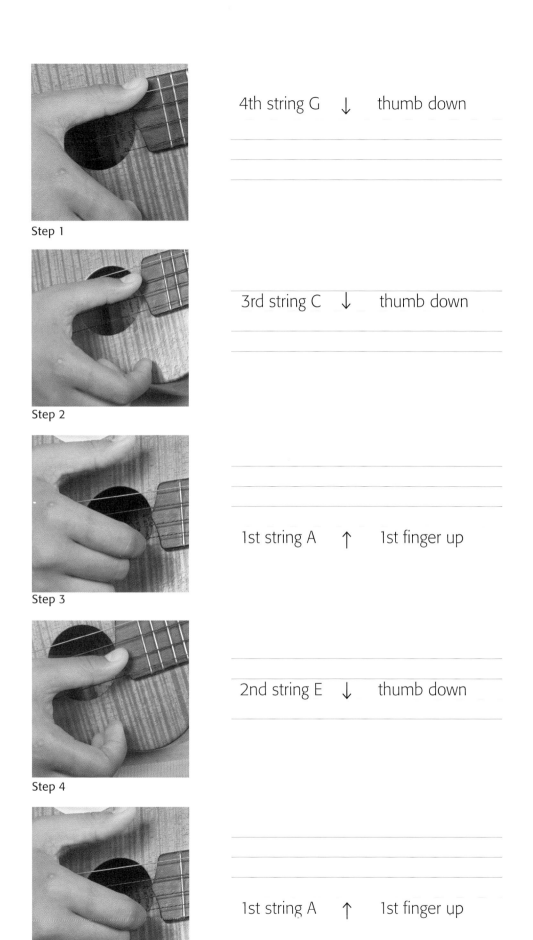

Step 1

4th string G   ↓   thumb down

Step 2

3rd string C   ↓   thumb down

Step 3

1st string A   ↑   1st finger up

Step 4

2nd string E   ↓   thumb down

Step 5

1st string A   ↑   1st finger up

Using the new finger-picking pattern for 3/4 and 6/8 time, accompany yourself on this classic melody with Hawaiian lyrics. Listen to the CD to hear how the picking fits to the beat.

 CD track 41

PŌ LA'I Ē

SILENT NIGHT

Traditional

Pō - la -'i ē, Po - ka - ma -ha'o!

Ma - lu - hia, Ma - la - ma - la - ma,

Ka - ma - kua hi - ne a - lo - ha e!

Me ke kei - ki he - mo - le - le e!

Moe me ma - lu - hia la - ni!

Moe me ka ma - lu - hia la - ni!

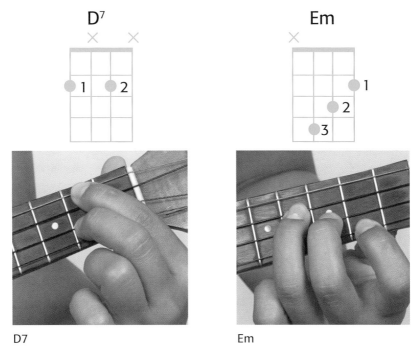

D7

Em

Use these chords along with the other G major chords to strum accompaniment in 3/4 time to this well-known Maori farewell song from New Zealand. It is also sung in Hawai'i.

CD track 42

NOW IS THE HOUR

New Zealand Traditional

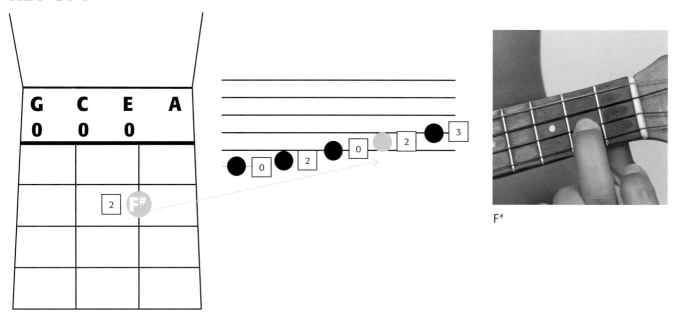

F#

The key of G major, which you have been playing in this lesson, has its special key signature. When you see this you will know to use the chords of the G major family.

E minor is the relative key to G major and so has the same key signature.
(In Lesson 7 you will learn the E minor sequence.)

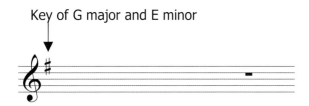

Key of G major and E minor

When you see that you are playing in the key of G or E minor, you will know not only which chords to use, but also that when you pick a melody you must play the F# on the 2nd fret.

Here are two exercises before you try picking a melody in the key of G major.

CD track 43

EXERCISE IN G MAJOR WITH F#

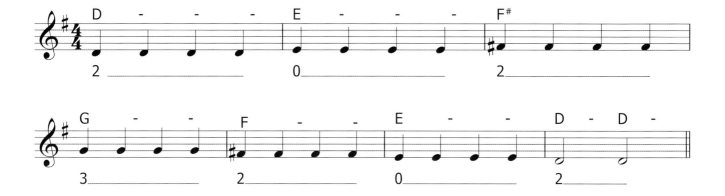

FRÈRE JACQUES—VARIATION
BROTHER JOHN

THE USE OF TREMOLO ON THE HAWAIIA A 'UKULELE

A violinist can make a note last a long time by drawing the bow slowly over a string.
For plucked instruments the only way to 'sustain' a note is to rapidly repeat it. This is called **tremolo**. Tremolo is an extremely important part of melodic playing on the 'ukulele, as it is on the mandolin, banjo, balalaika, or bouzouki, to name just a few folk instruments.

Most Hawaiian musicians who play melody use tremolo, and nearly all Hawaiian professional musicians do this with the right thumbnail, which has been allowed to grow to act as a natural pick. However, it is possible to play tremolo without having a long thumbnail! You need to buy a relatively soft or flexible pick, just a little stiffer than a yoghurt lid. In the islands of Vanuatu, I have seen parrot-fish scales used as picks!

See the pictures below how to hold the pick. Your hand should be relaxed, and the thumb holding the pick should be parallel to the strings. Again, make sure your pick is flexible.

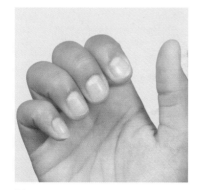

Start with your right hand vertical
with your thumbnail facing you.

Picture 1

Place the pick 3/4 way between
the thumb and index finger.

Picture 2

Now, in regular strumming position, hold the pick just above the strings. Lower it about 1/8 inch 'into' the strings when you begin to tremolo the notes.

Keep your thumb relaxed and parallel to the strings. Don't let your grip become claw-like and tense. Some players prefer to pivot the hand on the little finger.

Picture 3

EXERCISES TO DEVELOP TREMOLO SKILL

The timing of each exercise progresses so that you have to move to the
next note a little quicker. Each exercise has a repeat sign, so do each one twice.

When you have completed these exercises you should be ready to apply tremolo to a melody.

TREMOLO PRACTICE

Using the C Scale, tremolo each note to the count of Four.

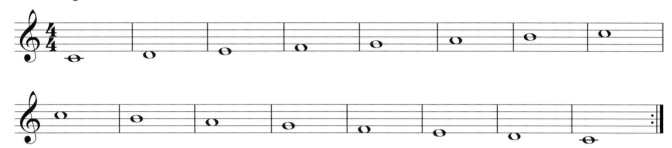

Tremolo each note to the count of Three, waltz time.

Tremolo each note to the count of Two, two notes per bar.

To finish this lesson pick the melody of *Now Is the Hour.*
This is a melody that definitely needs tremolo to sustain all the long notes in it.
Get familiar with just picking the notes by finger first. When you feel ready, use tremolo.

Listen to the CD to hear how it goes first.  CD track 46

Use tremolo to play *Now Is the Hour.*

NOW IS THE HOUR

New Zealand Traditional

Now is the hour_____ for us to say good-bye._____

Soon you'll be sail- ing far a-cross the sea._____ And

while you're a-way,_____ oh, friend, re-mem-ber me._____

When you re-turn, you'll find me wait - ing here._____

Lesson 7

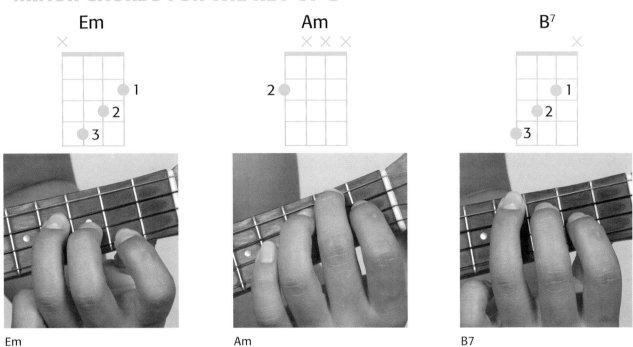

MINOR CHORDS FOR THE KEY OF G

Em

Am

B⁷

Em

Am

B7

Strum these new chords in the same sequence (see pages 13 and 14).

THE ROLL STRUM

This is one of the most important strum techniques used in Hawaiian 'ukulele playing. It is a colorful way of creating energy in the strum by rapidly striking the strings with the fingernails to create emphasis in the rhythm.

1. Start with the right hand relaxed and gently closed just above the 4th string.

2. Bring the hand down while opening the fingers. At the same time strike the strings starting with the 4th fingernail, progressing to the last, the index finger.

3. Make sure the hand uncurls like a fan and the fingernails strike the strings one after another.

Nearly all beginners have trouble with this because, at first, the four fingernails strum more or less as a single sound. This is incorrect. Listen to the CD to hear how it should sound on the C chord. CD track 48

THE ROLL STRUM (CONTINUED)

To get the correct sound you must hit the strings in a rapid roll.
It takes practice and the development of a little extra muscle power!
Imagine you are flicking something off your leg that needs a little force.
The other clue is that your hand should be properly open when you finish,
with the fingers more or less extended straight.

Incorrect finishing position

Correct finishing position

If you do not succeed immediately, try this:
Treat the inside of your open left-hand fingers as the four strings.
Tilt the hand away from you and practice roll strumming on your fingers.
At the end of the strum, your right hand should show its back much more
clearly than at the beginning when the hand is poised to go downward.
Now hold the simplest chord, C, and try roll strumming it.

Once you hear you are getting the right sound, practice chord groups counting and strumming
like this:

A single roll ~ followed by three down-strums and repeat for each chord.

~   two   three   four   / Practice this with your easiest chord sequence:
Roll   strum   strum   strum / C, F, G⁷, C

Listen to the CD to hear how it goes.   CD track 49

This strum takes time to master but it is really worth learning. If you get a muffled sound at first,
don't be discouraged. With practice it will get clearer and stronger!

Try other chord progressions you have learned using the same pattern:

F, B♭, C⁷   Am, Dm, E⁷   Dm, Gm, A⁷   G, C, D⁷   Em, Am, B⁷

For variation, strum in 3/4 time repeated before changing chords.   CD track 50

/ ~   two   three   /   ~   two   three   /
/ Roll   strum,   strum, /   Roll   strum,   strum,   /

NOTES ABOVE HIGH C

Here are two more notes enabling you to play above high C. The D can be played with the fourth finger if that is as high as the tune goes. If the melody goes higher to E or above, then you will need to play in a 'position.' This means the first finger will be put on the B or the C and you play up from there. To be technical, if your first finger begins on the second note B, then you are playing in second position. If the first finger starts on the third note, C, you are playing in third position.

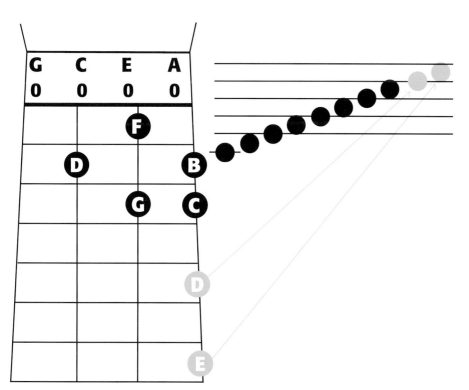

High D in 2nd position, use 3rd finger.

High E in 2nd position, use 4th finger.

Here are some exercises.  CD track 51

PRACTICE WITH HIGH D AND E

HOT CROSS BUNS—VARIATION

Try this classic round by Purcell. The third line part will need more practice. The piece is played peacefully and evenly. If you have two or three players they can come in at II and III. This is a lovely ensemble piece.

Try the beautiful chord sequence too. It is repeated in each section (I, II, III). CD track 52

THREE-PART ROUND

Henry Purcell

Lesson 7

BRINGING TOGETHER YOUR SKILLS

You have built up several skills: chord playing, sight-reading,
the beginning of tremolo, and the roll strum. These will all be called for on this page!

1. Practice chord sequences of G, D⁷, C and Em, Am, B⁷ by strumming in 3/4 time.
2. Strum them with a roll strum at the beginning of each chord:
~ 2, 3 /   ~2, 3 /

CD track 53

3. Accompany *Amazing Grace* using this same ~ 2, 3 / ~ 2, 3 / rhythm.
4. Pick the melody and use tremolo on all the notes worth more than one beat.

If you have someone to play with, alternate between picking
and strumming the accompaniment!

CD track 54

AMAZING GRACE

Lesson 8

THE KEY OF D

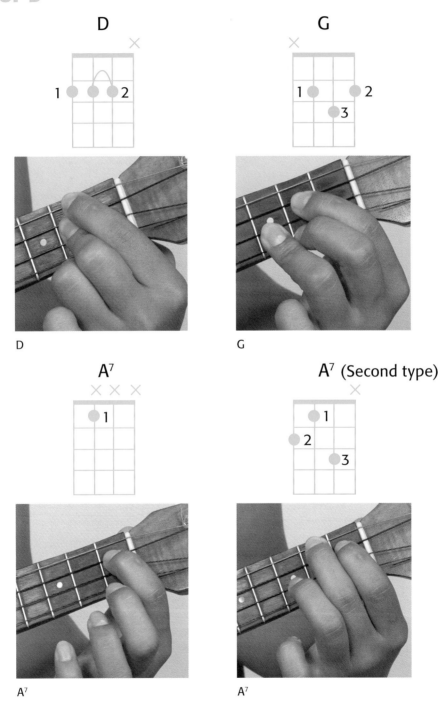

Practice these in the 8,6,4,3,2,1 sequence.
Use roll strums on the first beat if you can!
Note: Use only one of the A^7 types in the sequence and remember to end with a D chord.

STRUM RHYTHMS—ADDING VARIATIONS

A good musician will often vary the strum rhythm within a single tune,
though always keeping the beat.
If you just strum a regular 4/4 beat, **One, Two, Three, Four,** there is no variation.

A very common element in Hawaiian 'ukulele playing is the dotted beat or 'bounce' strum.
Here is a simple example: **/ One, Two-and Three, Four / One, Two-and Three, Four /**
(Use this rhythm with each of the chords above). CD track 55

Do the same with this rhythm. CD track 56

Here is another 'bounce' rhythm: **One, Two, Three-and Four / One, Two, Three-and Four /**

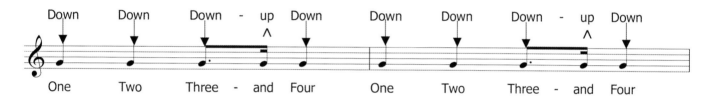

This next rhythm is not only 'bounced'
but also **syncopated**. Use the chords above. CD track 57

Syncopation happens when you don't strum one of the down-beats,
but holding off just a fraction, play the next up-beat. In this strum rhythm,
it is just before the 'and Four' of each bar.

A FAMOUS CALYPSO—*JAMAICA FAREWELL*—IN THE KEY OF D

This is an excellent example of the syncopated rhythm just explained.

Before playing the tune, listen to the CD and strum the new chord sequence to this rhythm. When you feel comfortable with the chords and the rhythm, try accompanying the song. CD track 58

JAMAICA FAREWELL

Lord Burgess

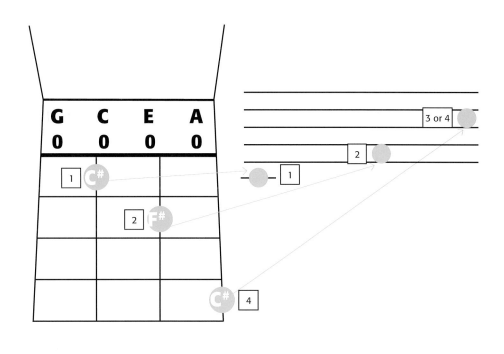

Low C#

High C#

The Key of D

You have been playing in this key in *Jamaica Farewell*.
It has two sharps: C# and F#. When you see a key signature with
these you will know to use the chords of the D major family.
B minor is the relative key to D major and so has the same
key signature. If the highest note you play is high C#,
use the 4th finger.

If you go up to high D use the 3rd for C# to leave the 4th free for D.

SCALE OF D MAJOR

Play this scale in waltz time first.

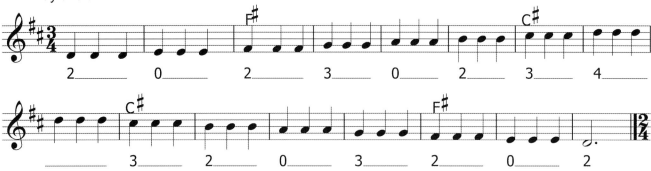

Now play in 2/4 or march time without note names or numbers.

Finally, play the D major scale in march time with no repeated notes.

The rhythm is the same as *Jamaica Farewell*. Notice the chord of A is introduced next to A⁷ in two measures. It is a very easy chord to learn as it is hardly any different in shape from A⁷.

WATER COME A ME EYE

Jamaica Traditional

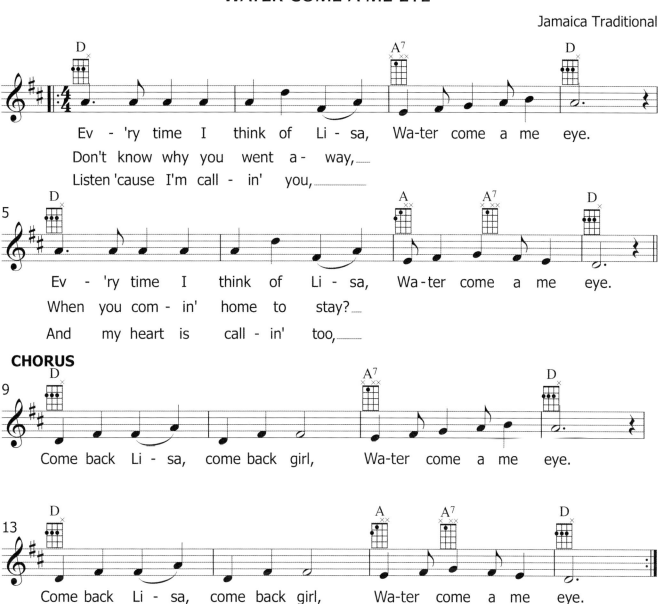

Now try to pick this song. You can add two touches:
1. Strum the D chord at the end of each line.
2. In the chorus, for the words: 'Come back Lisa, come back girl,' pluck pairs of strings of the D chord to play the melody, like this:

Come (4, 3) **back Li** (3, 2 / 3, 2) **sa** (2, 1) **Come** (4, 3) **back girl** (3, 2 / 3, 2)

Listen again!  CD track 60

There are only 12 letters in the Hawaiian alphabet,
the vowels **a, e, i, o, u,** and the consonants **h, k, l, m, n, p,** and **w.**

There is also the 'okina or glottal stop. It sounds like the way we say 'oh-oh,' when nervous!
The glottal stop signifies where a letter or letters have been left out. For example,
Hawai'i was originally **Hawai ik i.**

Generally, vowels are pronounced as follows:

a, as in f**a**ther
e, as in sl**ei**gh
i, as in myst**i**que
o, as in fl**o**w
u, as in r**u**le

All words and syllables end in vowels. This makes Hawaiian, like Italian,
a beautiful language to sing in!

Vowels together

If you see **ai** as in **kai** (sea), it is **not** pronounced as **ay** in **say** but as the sound **ah-ee** in **sigh**.
If you see **ou** as in **kou** (your), it is **not** pronounced as **ow** in **cow** but as the sound **oh** in **flow**.

The rule is: Pronounce each vowel purely as above.
If you see two vowels together then pronounce them one after the other.

ai is pronounced **ah-ee**

Consonants

It is very interesting that in Tahiti and New Zealand the **t** is sounded, whereas in
Hawai'i there is no **t** and the sound is transformed to a **k**. So, **Tahiti** is called **Kahiki** in Hawaiian.
Tapa cloth is called **kapa** cloth in Hawaiian. **Tapu** in Tahitian is **kapu** (forbidden) in Hawaiian.

The **r** in Tahitian and Maori is likewise changed, to **l** in Hawaiian.
Aroha in Maori is transformed to **aloha** in Hawaiian.

Another difference is the **w** pronunciation. In Hawaiian, it is usually pronounced as a **v** inside a
word. For example, the girl's name **Kawena** is pronounced **Kavena**. **If the w is at the beginning
it will be pronounced as a w.** In a fast flow of words, however, if a word beginning with **w** is in
the middle of a phrase, then it can become a **v**!

In New Zealand, the Maoris pronounce the **wh** (as it written in English approximation) very close
to the **f** sound. So the place **Whangerei** is pronounced **Fangerei**.

POKAREKARE ANA

Maori Traditional

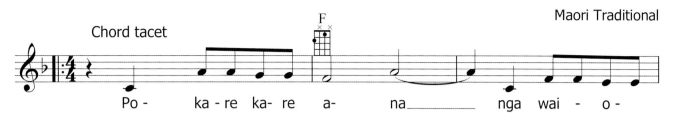

Po - ka - re ka - re a- na_____ nga wai - o -

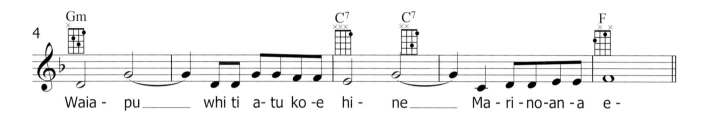

Waia - pu_____ whi ti a- tu ko- e hi - ne_____ Ma - ri -no-an -a e -

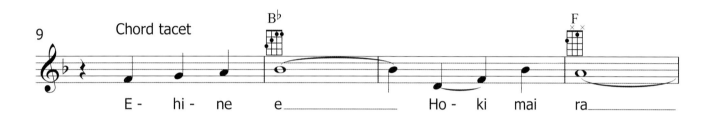

E - hi - ne e_____ Ho - ki mai ra_____

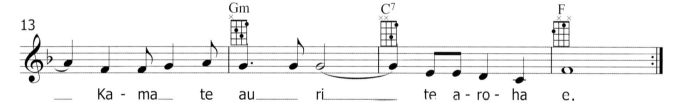

_____ Ka - ma_____ te au_____ ri_____ te a - ro - ha e.

More About Picking and Strumming

As you become more comfortable with sight-reading and also with your chords, you will want to bring these two sides of 'ukulele playing together in one place—the performance of any song.

Nearly all folk tunes have been built out of chord sequences. Some are composed so closely to the chords that by playing the notes in the chords you can practically play the tune. *Water Come a Me Eye* is a good example. In the following lessons you will find that the melody of the beautiful Hawaiian song *Pua Lililehua* sits wonderfully inside the chord sequence.

There are two main ways to bring chords and melody together,
1. When a note is held, usually at the end of a phrase you have time to strum the chord, especially if the chord's top note is the same as the melody note.
2. Some notes in a chord can be used to create the melody.

Chord Tacet: **Hold off strumming in this section.**

Strum along until you know the song. On the next page we will look at parts of it to enrich.

POKAREKARE ANA IN 4/4 TIME

Pokarekare Ana is often played in waltz time but this version is in 4/4 time.

Like the two calypso songs, the syncopated strum fits this song nicely. Below is the slightly altered version. Note that after the beginning down-beat, you syncopate the next beat.

As you pick the melody you can add this strum rhythm at the end of the phrases with notes that are three or more beats in length (see the wavy underlines). So after **a-**, on the **na__** you'll play the second part of the strum **up-down-up** and then the **down** because the note carries on into the first beat of the next bar.

CD track 62

POKAREKARE ANA

Maori Traditional

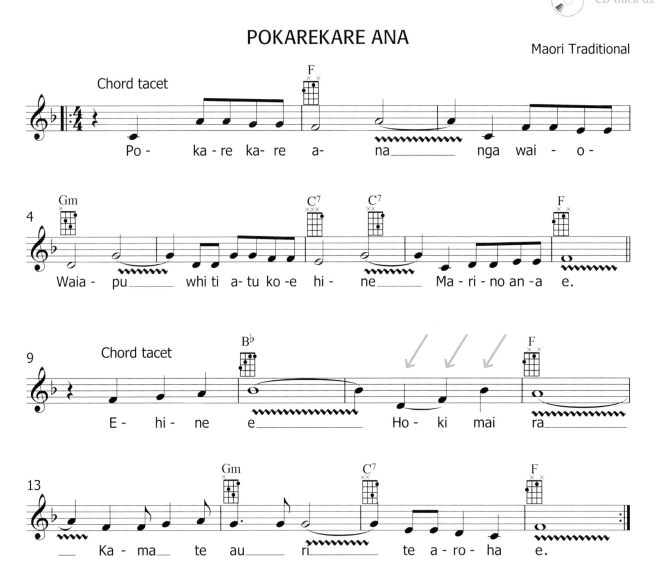

You can also add to your picking of the melody by using the chord as part of the melody itself. Try roll strumming the B♭ with the same rhythm pattern following and then, still keeping the fingers on the B♭ chord, pick the three notes (see arrows) **D, F, B♭ (Ho-ki mai)** on strings 3, 2, 1. The secret is to look for chances to use some of the chord notes to create the melody.

Lesson 9

KEYS OF B♭ AND G MINOR

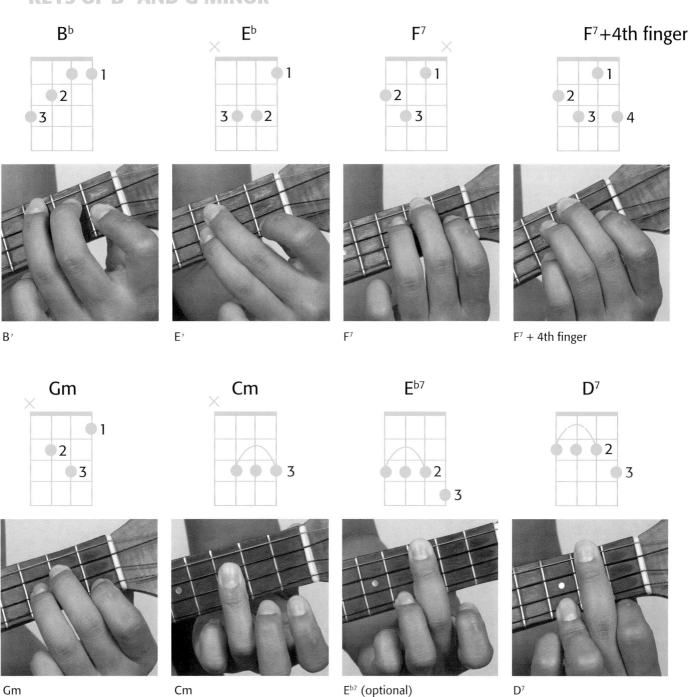

B♭   E♭   F⁷   F⁷+4th finger

B♭   E♭   F⁷   F⁷ + 4th finger

Gm   Cm   E♭⁷   D⁷

Gm   Cm   E♭⁷ (optional)   D⁷

Use the 8, 6, 4, 3, 2, 1 practice sequence to learn these chord progressions.
Although you will not play in the keys of B♭ and Gm very often, these chords appear
in other keys. Try your hand at the very charming 1919 song *I'm Forever Blowing Bubbles*.
It has very satisfying chord changes. Play it in a gentle waltz rhythm.

I'M FOREVER BLOWING BUBBLES

Jan Kenbrovin

Lesson 9

Any chord, higher up, can play a new chord.

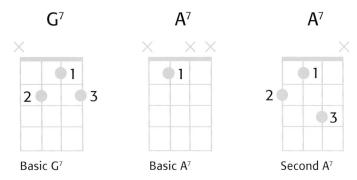

Basic G⁷   Basic A⁷   Second A⁷

F⁷ formation in two different positions:

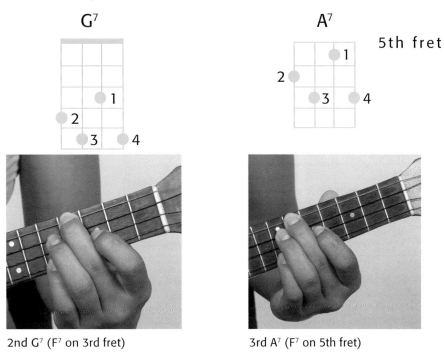

2nd G⁷ (F⁷ on 3rd fret)   3rd A⁷ (F⁷ on 5th fret)

Here is an example of how moving a chord up works for the D⁷ chord.

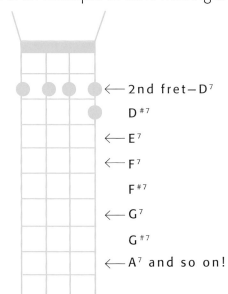

← 2nd fret–D⁷

D#⁷

← E⁷

← F⁷

F#⁷

← G⁷

G#⁷

← A⁷ and so on!

By shifting up a fret at a time, using the same pattern, you will get the 7th chord of each fret above the D⁷ home chord. A new G⁷, for example, using the D⁷ pattern, is formed on the 7th fret.

In *I'm Forever Blowing Bubbles*, the final F⁷ is played in this formation on the 5th fret. In the next song, we will add a high G⁷ using the D⁷ chord on the 7th fret.

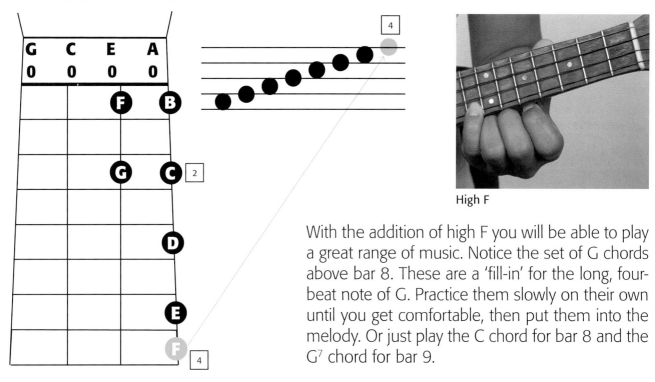

High F

With the addition of high F you will be able to play a great range of music. Notice the set of G chords above bar 8. These are a 'fill-in' for the long, four-beat note of G. Practice them slowly on their own until you get comfortable, then put them into the melody. Or just play the C chord for bar 8 and the G⁷ chord for bar 9.

Play along with the CD until you are familiar with the tune and then try to pick it using tremolo for the long notes.

CD track 64

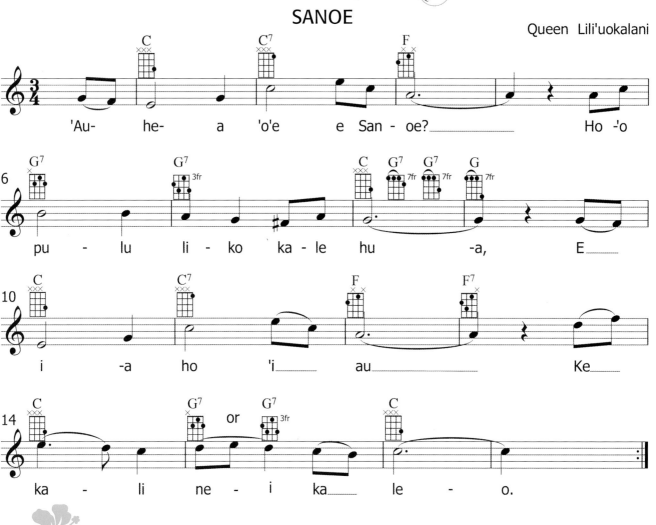

SANOE

Queen Lili'uokalani

'Au- he- a 'o'e e San- oe?_____ Ho -'o

pu - lu li - ko ka- le hu -a, E_____

i -a ho 'i____ au____ Ke____

ka - li ne- i ka___ le - o.

Lesson 9

Lesson 10

THE TRIPLET STRUM

'Ukulele strumming gets a lot more colorful if you are able add triplet rhythms. The triplet is very common in folk music in many places, especially Irish dance music, which is highly rhythmical.

If we strum a 4/4 beat, the triplet can be put on any beat, but more usually on the **third beat**.

It will sound like this:

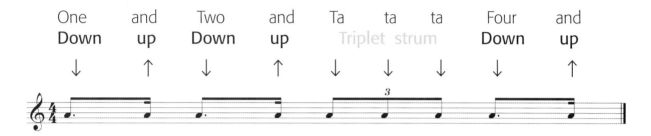

One	and	Two	and	Ta	ta	ta	Four	and
Down	**up**	**Down**	**up**	Triplet	strum		**Down**	**up**
↓	↑	↓	↑	↓	↓	↓	↓	↑

To achieve the triplet, which has to fit in three strums in one beat, do the following:

1. Strum down with just the index finger.

2. The thumb follows just behind and rolls across the strings.

3. Up-strum straight after, with your index finger.

4. Continue with the down-up of the index finger.

Use the C chord. Start very slowly and step by step get quicker.  CD track 65

When you have become more confident in picking and tremolo, you can come back to this tune and learn to play the melody as well.

LIVE ALOHA

M. Preston

Vanuatu Traditonal

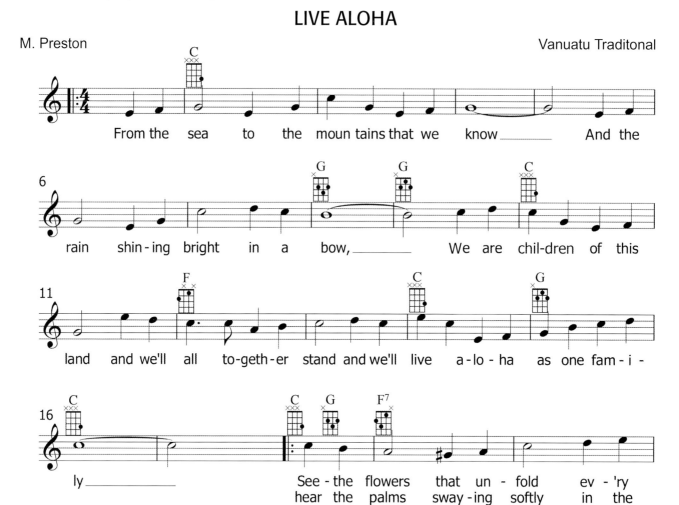

From the sea to the moun-tains that we know_____ And the

rain shin-ing bright in a bow,_____ We are chil-dren of this

land and we'll all to-geth-er stand and we'll live a-lo-ha as one fam-i-

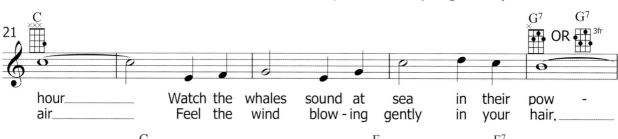

ly_____

See the flowers that un-fold ev-'ry
hear the palms sway-ing softly in the

hour_____ Watch the whales sound at sea in their pow -
air_____ Feel the wind blow-ing gently in your hair._____

er. We are chil-dren of this land and well all to-geth er stand and we'll

live a-lo-ha as one fam-i-ly_____

FURTHER TRIPLET STRUM SKILLS

The triplet strum can be used in all kinds of combinations. Here are some further suggestions.

↓ ↓ ↑   ↓ ↓ ↑

Triplet - down-up / Triplet - down-up / Hear how it goes!

Try this pattern on different chord sequences you have already mastered.

To start, take the chords of C major and A minor:

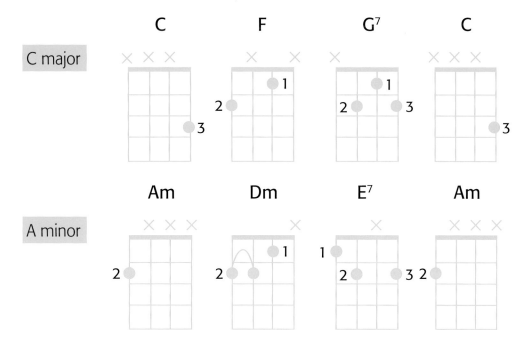

Now try with the chords of F major and D minor:

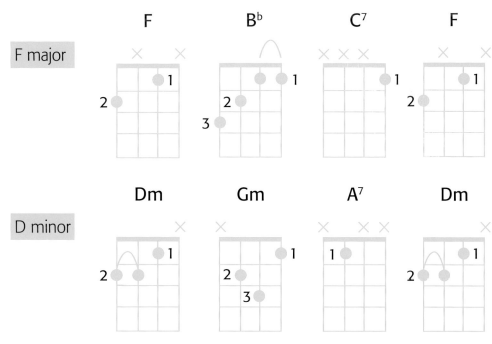

ANOTHER VERY USEFUL STRUMMING TECHNIQUE: USE THE THUMB AND INDEX FINGER

The thumb gives the first and third beats and the index finger strums up and down the extra beats.

One (thumb down on 4th string)

and Two and (index up/down/up on the other three strings)

Three (thumb down on 4th string)

and Four and (index up/down/up on the other three strings)

Try this 'finger' rhythm with some of the chord sequences on page 75.
You will need to support your hand on the little finger below the strings, between the bridge and the sound hole. It will act as a steadier and pivot (see picture below).

CD track 68

Little finger as a pivot.

When you are comfortable with the basic thumb-finger strum, a challenge is to add a **triplet**. The triplet can come on the 2nd or 4th beat.

You rapidly move the index finger four times instead of three for the triplet.

On the 2nd or 4th beat the strum will be: **Up**/down/up/down. Or, expressed another way, **Up** followed by a quick triplet.

CD track 69

This beautiful tune has a second, falsetto part. If there are two or more players you can take turns on each part. A third player can strum.

PUA LILILEHUA

Kahauanu Lake

Vamp: The Hawaiian vamp is a series of chords, usually three, strummed as a bridge between verses.

Fine: It means final measure to end the piece.

This charming song tells of the watchful little plover of Kekaha on Kaua'i.
Legend has it that the spirits of the departed leave from here to the next world.

CD track 71

'ŪLILI Ē
THE GOLDEN PLOVER OF KEKAHA

Traditional

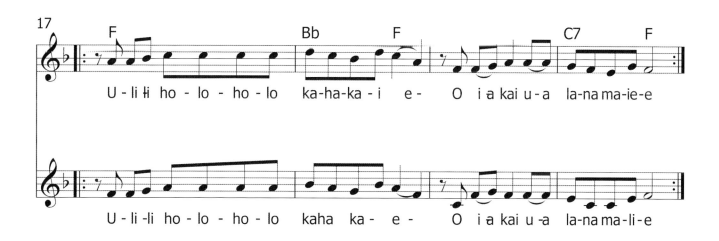

The melody is sometimes played and sung in 'dotted' or bounce rhythm.
If you play it this way, then the thumb-finger strum is excellent and you
can also add triplets. To hear it played this way, listen to the CD.

CD track 72

CRAZY G

Traditional

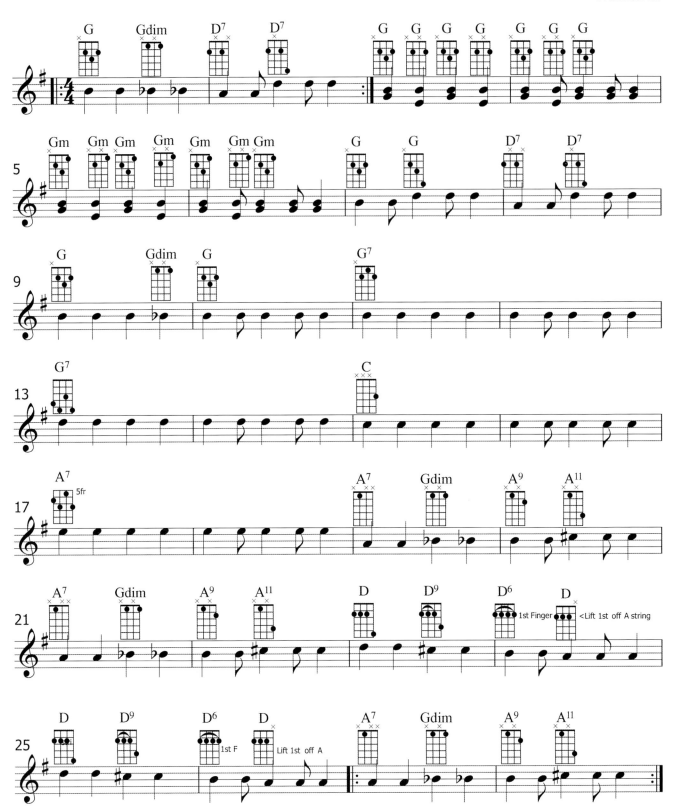

Lesson 10

This is a wonderful solo piece played entirely from chords, perfect for the roll and triplet strum! It is built from just two rhythms:

1. Four straight beats to the bar—**Down/down/down/down**
2. A second, syncopated rhythm—**Down/down-up/-up/down**

Feel free to extemporize with the strums!

(Special thanks to Roy Sakuma for this version of *Crazy G.*)

CD track 73

It is fitting to end with *Hawaiʻi Aloha*, one of Hawaiʻi's best-loved songs, sung at the end of many ceremonies with all participants in a circle holding hands. All over Hawaiʻi, children sing it for May Day. There are many ways to strum this. A double-beat strum (8 strums to the bar) is very effective. Use the roll strum for emphasis in certain places. For picking the melody, use tremolo for the long notes.

CD track 74

HAWAIʻI ALOHA

Makua Laīana
(Rev. Lorenzo Lyons)

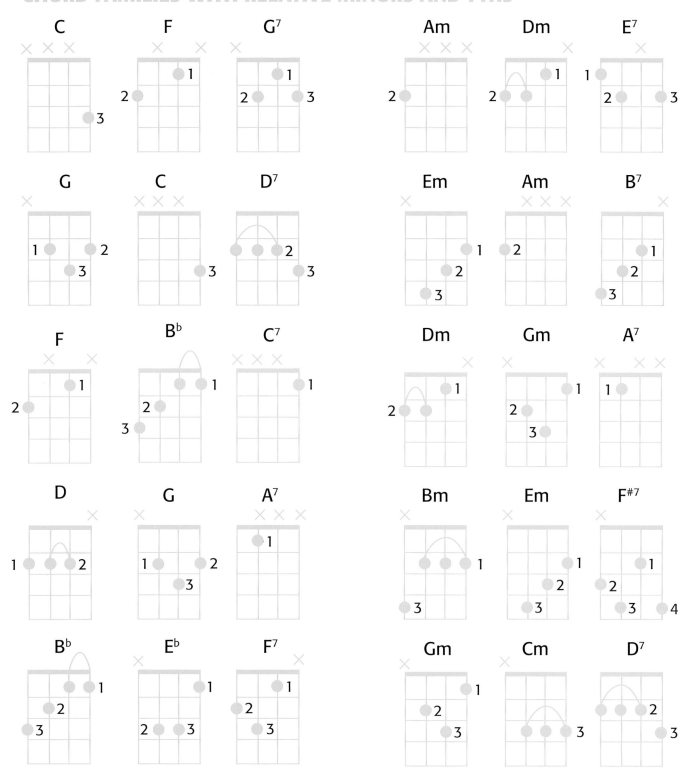

As you go through the book, use the families you know as warm-ups to practice different kinds of strumming rhythms.

Remember, for strumming practice, all families end on the home or starting chord. C F G⁷ ends with the C chord, Am–Dm–E⁷ ends with the Am chord, and so on. When you reach the end of the book you should be able to play all of these chords! For further reference, a bigger, 'dictionary'-type list of chords is also included.

'Ukulele Chord Chart

A

A	A⁷	Am	Am⁷

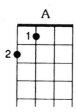 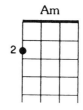

A♯ /B♭

A♯/B♭	A♯⁷/B♭⁷	A♯m/B♭m	A♯m⁷/B♭m⁷

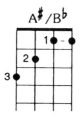 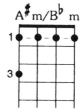

B

B	B⁷	Bm	Bm⁷

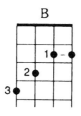 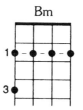

C

C	C⁷	Cm	Cm⁷

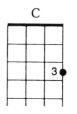 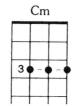 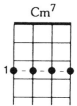

C♯ /D♭

C♯/D♭	C♯⁷/D♭⁷	C♯m/D♭m	C♯m⁷/D♭m⁷

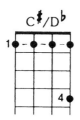 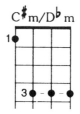 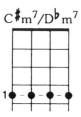

D

D	D⁷	Dm	Dm⁷

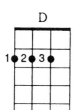 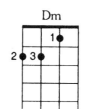 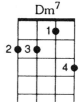

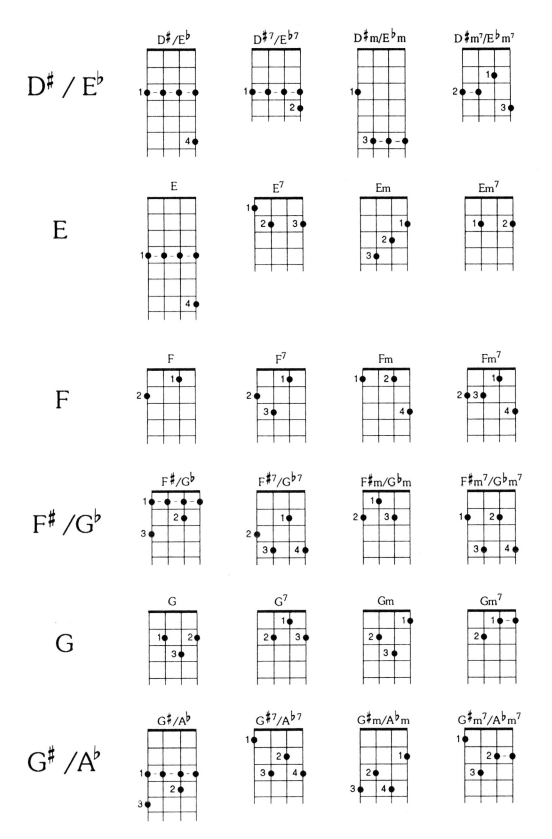

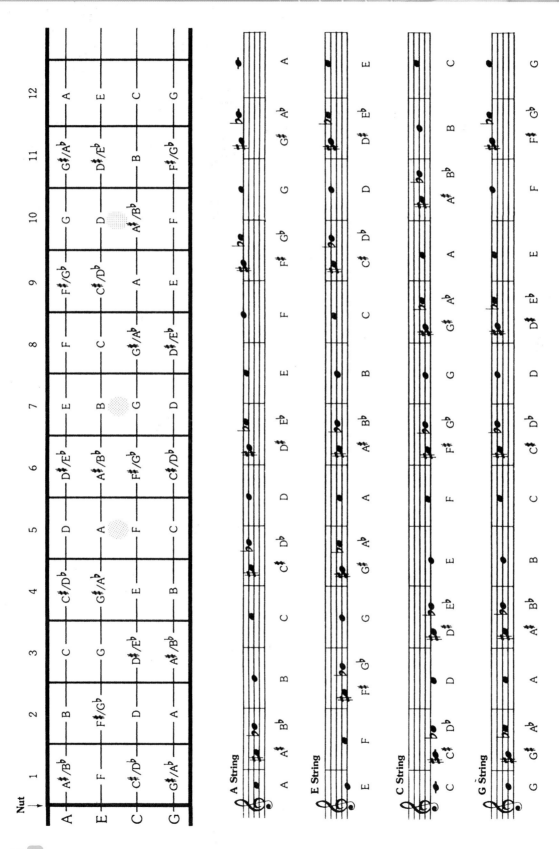